Kingdom Scribes
Seeking the Scribes Anointing

How do ye say, We are wise, and
the law of the LORD is with us? Lo,
certainly in vain made he it; the
pen of the scribes is in vain.

Jeremiah 8:8

So I opened my mouth, and he
caused me to eat that roll.

And he said unto me, Son of man,
cause thy belly to eat, and fill thy
bowels with this roll that I give
thee. Then did I eat it; and it was in
my mouth as honey for sweetness.

Ezekiel 3:1-3

Also by M. J. Welcome

Taking Captivity Captive

I am Powerful, Supported & respected

Transitioning into Fullness

I AM Loving, Lovable & Loved

Breathe Easy Coaching for Christians Growing in Love

Overcome Secret Sins in 15 Days

Battling for the Light

The 21-Day Crucifixion Challenge

Understanding the Power of God's Word

Seeking Total Restoration

Spiritual Diseases of the Unbridled Tongue

Mustard Seed Pocket Prayers of Renewal

Order books at Amazon
HTTPS://WWW.AMAZON.COM/
Visit my Author page
AMAZON.COM/AUTHOR/MICHELLEJWELCOME
AMAZON.COM/AUTHOR/MJWELCOME

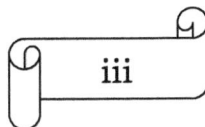

KINGDOM SCRIBES

Seeking the
Scribes Anointing

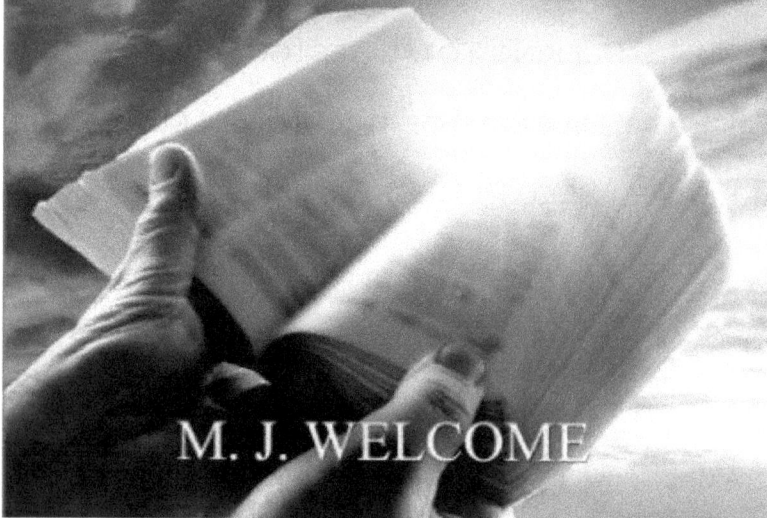

M. J. WELCOME

Smart Publishing House
A Division of MDW Consulting Group
Far Rockaway, New York
WWW.SMARTPUBLISHINGHOUSE.COM

Editing | Layout S.M.A.R.T Copy Designs
Proofreader | Matteel Welcome

S.M.A.R.T Copy Designs
WWW.SMARTCOPYDESIGNSINC.COM

First Published by Smart Publishing House
03/25/19

Library of Congress Control Number: 2016911810
ISBN-10:0-9825400-8-6
ISBN-13:978-0-9825400-8-4

Note: This publication is intended to provide helpful information on the subject matter covered. It is sold with the understanding that the author and publisher are not rendering professional services in the book. This book is a study guide to help the reader expand his knowledge of the Word of God.

Printed in the U.S.A.

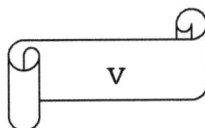

ACKNOWLEDGEMENTS & THANK YOU

Praise Jehovah who saw it fit to birth this book for the scribes of His Kingdom! Praise Him for he has placed a unique calling on our lives. Rejoice in him for He has ordained us for generational and eternal impact. Glorify Him for He placed something *exceptional* in us that only we can do and fulfill.

Lord, I thank you and rejoice in you. I glorify you for you are a wonderful God. Your lessons are in all that you do. Your support is woven into all that you have made known. Lord, there is no one else like you. I praise you for calling me to be a Kingdom Scribe. I bless you for the Scribes Anointing! Thank you Jesus, the Son of the Most High God!

To my family Dwain, Maheem, and Matteel, thank you for your support and encouragement as I labored to birth this work. Matteel, a special thank you for being my helper in this and on so many other projects! You are a gem and I pray blessings upon you for your generosity toward me.

To Pastors Fuloso and Toyin Akinbola, thank you so much for continually praying with me over each book. Thank you for your encouragement and support. I appreciate and celebrate you. God has blessed us with you and we are thankful.

Coleen Norris, thank you for your willingness to pray and read over my book projects. I appreciate the jokes and the words of encouragement! You have been a blessing to me and I thank God for our friendship!

Thank you Scribe for purchasing *Kingdom Scribes, Seeking the Scribes Anointing*! May the anointing of God be increased in your life. May he increase the works of your hands and cause you to birth many spiritual babies to his honor and glory. My prayer is that as you study the scribes of old that you will be encouraged, strengthened and challenged.

As you learn of them, I pray that you will glean deeper insights into our awesome God. Jehovah leaves nothing to chance, all is planned, and everything is ordained according to the counsel of his will. Therefore, your choosing to read this book at this time is not a coincidence! May you get all he has prepared for you with increase in Jesus' name.

Thank you again!

Your fellow Kingdom Scribe,
Who's continually *Seeking the Scribes Anointing*

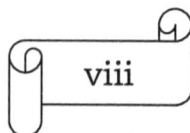

This devotional is designed to enable and encourage believers to walk confidently in their calling as *kingdom scribes* under the anointing of God as fierce warriors of Christ.

A *scribe* is one who recounts with accuracy or relates information exactly as given. He rehearses and declares what he is told and functions in the capacity of a secretary, muster-officer (one who takes an account of troops), or an enumerator (a person who takes a census of a population).

When we examine the root meaning for the word *scribe*, we discover that he's a public servant, a learned man, one who can analyze the difficult and subtle questions of law. Furthermore, he's a religious teacher with the ability to commit things to writing so that they are not forgotten. *Scribes* also give directions.

Therefore, a solemn charge has been given to scribes in the Kingdom of God. It is not for popularity, fame, or fortune that we write, but to advance the agenda of God as we battle for the light of Christ to be established in the hearts and minds of fallen men. It is for us to use His anointing to pierce the eye of the reader to the glory of God.

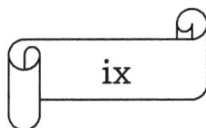

As we embark on this journey with the Lord, may we strive to obey his will and obtain increased anointing as we advance the call of God so that all who are willing may come!

Your fellow *scribe* in Christ Jesus,

M. J. Welcome

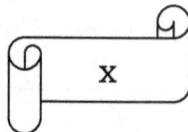

TABLE OF CONTENTS

ACKNOWLEDGEMENTS & THANK YOU VII

GREETINGS TO ALL KINGDOM SCRIBES...................... IX

SERAIAH THE SCRIBE 16

    WEEK 1 22

    WEEK 2 26

    PRAYER....................................... 27

    WEEK 3 30

    PRAYER....................................... 31

    WEEK 4 34

JONATHAN THE SCRIBE 38

    WEEK 1 43

    WEEK 2 47

    WEEK 3 50

    WEEK 4 54

SHEVA THE SCRIBE 58

    WEEK 1 63

    WEEK 2 67

    WEEK 3 71

    WEEK 4 75

JEIEL THE SCRIBE 78

    WEEK 1 85

    WEEK 2 89

    WEEK 3 94

    WEEK 4 98

ELISHAMA THE SCRIBE............................... 102

    WEEK 1 107

    WEEK 2 112

WEEK 3 116

PRAYER.. 117

WEEK 4 120

EZRA THE SCRIBE.. 124

WEEK 1 128

WEEK 2 131

WEEK 3 136

WEEK 4 141

PRAYER.. 142

SHIMSHAI THE SCRIBE 144

WEEK 1 147

WEEK 2 153

WEEK 3 157

WEEK 4 161

SHEBNA THE SCRIBE.. 164

WEEK 1 170

WEEK 2 175

WEEK 3 179

WEEK 4 183

BARUCH THE SCRIBE 186

WEEK 1 192

WEEK 2 197

WEEK 3 202

WEEK 4 207

ZADOK THE SCRIBE 210

WEEK 1 215

WEEK 2 220

WEEK 3 224

WEEK 4 229

Shavsha the Scribe 232

    Week 1 239

    Week 2 241

    Week 3 248

    Week 4 254

Shaphan the Scribe 258

    Week 1 263

    Week 2 268

    Week 3 273

    Week 4 279

Conclusion 281

Challenge 287

About Author 287

January

SERAIAH THE SCRIBE
Jehovah is Ruler

And Zadok the son of Ahitub, and
Ahimelech the son of Abiathar,
were the priests; and Seraiah was
the scribe;

2 Samuel 8:17

The LORD hath prepared his
throne in the heavens; and his
kingdom ruleth over all.

Psalm 103:19

Seraiah is a name that means, "Jehovah is ruler." Its meaning comes from two root words, one means to have power, to contend, to persevere. The other is Jehovah, "the existing one." The base meaning of Jehovah is to become, to exist, to fall, and to happen, to desire, wait, long for, wish, sigh, crave, lust, and to turn aside to lodge.

The Gesenius' Hebrew-Chaldee Lexicon gives the meaning of **Seraiah** as a "soldier of Jehovah".

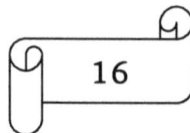

If we put everything together, we see that Jehovah causes things to be instituted, established, occur or to fall out of existence.

As scribes, we are soldiers of the Lord; therefore, we are tasked with ensuring that the purpose of God is fulfilled in our sphere of influence.

Psalm 103:19 tells us that the power, realm, and reign of God is *over everything without exception.* His counsel and advice is above that of any man; therefore, it is *superior in quality* and should not be taken lightly.

The Existing One has firmly established his seat of honor concealed in the lofty sky and his dominion as King is over **all**.

What does this mean for *us* as scribes?

It means that if we are willing, God will rule, give counsel, and exercise his power in our writing. He has the perfect position to see all therefore, he is able to guide what we do in order to ensure the best results. He will strategically teach us what we are to do to defend, uphold, and advance his kingdom.

Since God is over all he is to be honored as the most-high God!

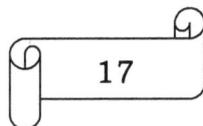

Unfortunately, most of us don't consistently honor God as the most-high God. Over the next *four* weeks, we will identify areas where God should be established as King and devise ways to seat him firmly on his throne in our lives.

Far above all principality, and power, and might, and dominion, and every name that is named, not only in this world, but also in that which is to come:

Ephesians 1:21

SERAIAH THE SCRIBE
Jehovah is Ruler

And Zadok the son of Ahitub, and
Ahimelech the son of Abiathar,
were the priests; and Seraiah was
the scribe;

2 Samuel 8:17

Week 1

The LORD hath prepared his
throne in the heavens; and his
kingdom ruleth over all.

Psalm 103:19

Hidden in the root meaning Seraiah's name is a key to Jehovah's rule. The Gesenius' Hebrew-Chaldee Lexicon states that the root meaning of Seraiah is to place in order, to put things in a row. It is to be a commander, prince and leader. It is to fight!

Our God is a commander, warrior, and an organizer. He puts things in order by strategic means. He determines what needs to be done by the counsel of his own will.

19

> In whom also we have obtained an inheritance, being predestinated according to the purpose of him who worketh all things after the counsel of his own will:
>
> Ephesians 1:11

God rules with perseverance, persistency, and power. He contends with those who contend with his children and by extension with him.

> But thus saith the LORD, Even the captives of the mighty shall be taken away, and the prey of the terrible shall be delivered: for I will contend with him that contendeth with thee, and I will save thy children.
>
> Isaiah 49:25

The purpose of God contending is to put things into order and to establish his rulership in the situation. As scribes, we should look to God to put things in order for us. We can contend for things ourselves; however, our ability to see and understand is limited while God has the best vantage point to ensure the most beneficial outcome.

For the kingdom is the LORD'S:
and he is the governor among the
nations.

Psalm 22:28

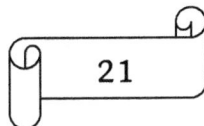

WEEK 1

Are there things in your writing experience that *you desire God to rule over or take charge of*?

For the LORD is our judge, the LORD is our lawgiver, the LORD is our king; he will save us.

Isaiah 33:22

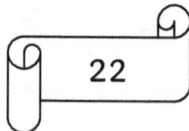

PRAYER

Jehovah, you are the one that causes things to be established. In my life, please help me to establish (**fill in what you need from the Lord**). Cause it to be firm and immovable. Help me as I train as a soldier of Jehovah to become skilled and proficient in the work you have assigned for me to do. In the name of Jesus, I ask these blessings, amen.

SERAIAH THE SCRIBE
Jehovah is Ruler

And Zadok the son of Ahitub, and
Ahimelech the son of Abiathar,
were the priests; and Seraiah was
the scribe;

2 Samuel 8:17

Week 2

The LORD hath prepared his
throne in the heavens; and his
kingdom ruleth over all.

Psalm 103:19

Jehovah's kingdom *ruleth over all*. What a glorious phrase and truth! God is over all. The word *kingdom* here means sovereign power, royal power, dominion, realm and to reign. At the root, it means to become king, to make one a king or queen, or to be a king or queen with the power to advise and to give counsel.

God's kingdom is established for the purpose of dominion. For him to exercise his royal and sovereign power over all with the specific goal of causing others to be like him. He wants to establish royal children who can rule as he rules.

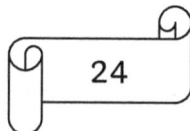

24

Kingdom Scribes
Seeking the Scribes Anointing

Yea, all kings shall fall down before him: all nations shall serve him.

Psalm 72:11

WEEK 2

In light of the fact that Jehovah's kingdom exists to raise up royal children, what declarations will you make in regard to your inheritance?

He made him lord of his house,

And ruler of all his possessions,

Psalm 105:21

PRAYER

Jehovah, you have called me as a scribe, and as your royal child to establish dominion wherever I go. Lord help me to be rooted in firmness. Help me to walk in truth. Help me to grow in understanding. Help me to call what is not as if it is. Lord, by faith, I declare (**list what you are declaring**). In the name of Jesus, I call it done, amen.

SERAIAH THE SCRIBE
Jehovah is Ruler

And Zadok the son of Ahitub, and
Ahimelech the son of Abiathar,
were the priests; and Seraiah was
the scribe;

2 Samuel 8:17

Week 3

The LORD hath prepared his
throne in the heavens; and his
kingdom ruleth over all.

Psalm 103:19

Jehovah **rules** with the purpose of assimilation.
He desires us to be like him. That is why he
gave dominion to man (Genesis 1:26) so that
we could learn how to rule as he rules. How does
Jehovah rule? What does he value most? How do
you rule yourself? Does it line up with what God
expects? Does it reflect the nature of God?

He rules by His power forever;

His eyes observe the nations;

Do not let the rebellious exalt themselves. Selah

Psalm 66:7

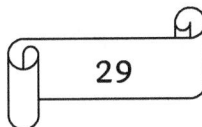

WEEK 3

As you ponder the questions above you may feel that there are blocks to you being all that God desires you to be. These are mountains. What mountains do you desire to see removed from your life? From your craft? From your family? Remember that, like a soldier, you grow in skill and precision as you practice in battle.

PRAYER

Jehovah you have given me dominion over (**list what he has given you dominion over**). I have fallen short and I ask your forgiveness. I desire to please you, to be like you, to be assimilated fully into the kingdom way. There are mountains that are in my way. I speak to the mountains of (**list them**) that ye be moved in the name of Jesus. I call forth (**name what you call forth**) to be established in my life, family, relationship, work, and writing in the name of Jesus, amen.

Seraiah the Scribe
Jehovah is Ruler

And Zadok the son of Ahitub, and
Ahimelech the son of Abiathar,
were the priests; and Seraiah was
the scribe;

2 Samuel 8:17

Week 4

The LORD hath prepared his
throne in the heavens; and his
kingdom ruleth over all.

Psalm 103:19

Scribe *Seraiah (YOU)*, Jehovah is ruler in your life. You are a soldier of the most high God. You have been given dominion over the works of your hand. You have power and authority over your life as well as what is established in it.

What things do you want to fall away? What things do you want to be established? Jehovah caused Satan and his angels to fall from heaven (Isaiah 14:12-15 and Ezekiel 28:12-19). Jesus made an open mockery of the works of Satan (Colossians 2:15). If Satan is contending with you, you must remember that your God is over all. He causes things to exist or to fall. You are a royal child in training. You have been given authority over all the works of the devil (Luke 10:19). Establish dominion. Holy Spirit is with you to ensure that you bring in the victory for God.

When the righteous are in authority, the people rejoice;

But when a wicked man rules, the people groan.

Proverbs 29:2

What tangible steps can you take to place Jehovah over your writing? Life? Ministry?

PRAYER

Jehovah, as you are over all be over my life. As you have established your dominion, may you help me to do the same in my life, family, and work. Let it be according to your divine order. Send me help to lay hold of what the enemy is contending with me for. Help me to grow in understanding and might. Help me to exercise wisdom and soundness of judgment. Lord, teach my mouth to speak with authority that yields eternal results in the name of Jesus, amen.

February

JONATHAN THE SCRIBE
Jehovah has given

Also Jonathan David's uncle was a counseller, a wise man, and a scribe: and Jehiel the son of Hachmoni was with the king's sons:

1 Chronicles 27:32

The heaven, even the heavens, are the LORD'S: but the earth hath he given to the children of men.

Psalm 115:16

The name **Jonathan** means, "Jehovah has given." As kingdom scribes, God has entrusted us with a wondrous opportunity to write for the kingdom. As such, we are expected to yield produce for the kingdom of God.

When we examine the root meaning of the name **Jonathan**, we discover that it means to *be published*. Therefore, as scribes, we are to publish things for the glory of God.

Kingdom Scribes
Seeking the Scribes Anointing

When the Lord gives us an idea, we are to invest it with the intent of increasing its value as in the parable of the talents. If we refuse to invest what God has entrusted to us, we are like the servant who buried his talent in the ground.

> Then he that had received the five talents went and traded with the same, and made them other five talents. And likewise he that had received two, he also gained other two.
>
> Matthew 25:16-17

What have you done with what God has given you?
What would the Lord call you? How would he categorize your actions?

> His lord answered and said unto him, Thou wicked and slothful servant, thou knewest that I reap where I sowed not, and gather where I have not strawed:
>
> Matthew 25:26

Therefore, as kingdom scribes, let us purpose in our hearts and minds to invest all that the Lord has given to us so that it will multiply and bless many for countless generations.

That ye might walk worthy of the Lord unto all pleasing, being fruitful in every good work, and increasing in the knowledge of God;

Colossians 1:10

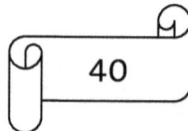

JONATHAN THE SCRIBE
Jehovah has given

Also Jonathan David's uncle was a
counseller, a wise man, and a
scribe: and Jehiel the son of
Hachmoni was with the king's
sons:

1 Chronicles 27:32

Week 1

The heaven, even the heavens, are
the LORD'S: but the earth hath he
given to the children of men.

Psalm 115:16

The heavens belong to the Lord. They are comprised of stars, the visible universe, the atmosphere and the sky. The lofty place that spreads out spanning from one side to another as a vault over the world. Supported by the foundation and columns of the Lord which he established by his Word (Colossians 1:17).

As he holds the heavens, he holds you. He has entrusted you with his plans for the earth (Mark 16:15).

And God blessed them, and God
said unto them, Be fruitful, and
multiply, and replenish the earth,
and subdue it: and have dominion
over the fish of the sea, and over
the fowl of the air, and over every
living thing that moveth upon the
earth.

Genesis 1:28

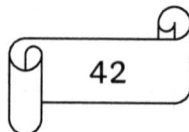

WEEK 1

What are the talents that the Lord has entrusted to you? How will you use them to go forth? How will you exercise dominion? How will you replenish the earth?

PRAYER

L ord, you have blessed me with the beauty of your creation. They testify of you. Lord help me to appreciate it more. Teach me through your creation, your faithfulness, might, splendor as well as your awesomeness, and your delight in divine order. Let me learn from you.

You have given to me (**list the things here**) so that I may be like you. That beauty and strength may be established. So that honor and glory can burst forth. So that seeds of holiness and purity can be sown in the hearts of men. Teach me as I sit at your feet. I am listening, amen.

JONATHAN THE SCRIBE
Jehovah has given

Also Jonathan David's uncle was a
counseller, a wise man, and a
scribe: and Jehiel the son of
Hachmoni was with the king's
sons:

1 Chronicles 27:32

Week 2

The heaven, even the heavens, are
the LORD'S: but the earth hath he
given to the children of men.

Psalm 115:16

The Lord has *given* to men the firm earth the ground that we walk upon, the regions that exist and the territories that are claimed. He has entrusted us with a portion of his creation. He permits us to till the ground, sow seeds, reap harvests, and produce goods.

A Psalm of David. The earth is the LORD'S, and the fulness thereof; the world, and they that dwell therein.

Psalm 24:1

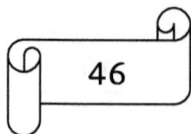

WEEK 2

What have you sown for the Lord? How fruitful is it? What do you need from God in order to be as he is? To be **abundant**?

PRAYER

As your scribe, teach me to sow seeds in the hearts and minds of men. Incorruptible seeds which will yield unto eternity. Endow me with a ready word and sound counsel. You have given me (**list what he has given you**). Lord, teach me how to care for it with soundness so that it will be firm and survive the time of testing in the name of Jesus.(1Corinthians 3:12-15).

Now if any man build upon this foundation gold, silver, precious stones, wood, hay, stubble;

Every man's work shall be made manifest: for the day shall declare it, because it shall be revealed by fire; and the fire shall try every man's work of what sort it is.

If any man's work abide which he hath built thereupon, he shall receive a reward.

If any man's work shall be burned, he shall suffer loss: but he himself shall be saved; yet so as by fire.

1 Corinthians 2:12-15

JONATHAN THE SCRIBE
Jehovah has given

Also Jonathan David's uncle was a counseller, a wise man, and a scribe: and Jehiel the son of Hachmoni was with the king's sons:

1 Chronicles 27:32

Week 3

The heaven, even the heavens, are the LORD'S: but the earth hath he given to the children of men.

Psalm 115:16

Psalms 115:16 states that God has given the earth to the children of men. The children of men includes our future generations (the just and the unjust a like). The purpose for which God entrusted us with the earth is so we can build and rebuild his house and family. This is the root meaning of *children*.

God desires to erect a monument to himself in which he can abide and dwell. How can you help God achieve his desire? What is it that you want to establish for future generations?

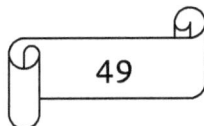

WEEK 3

What things are preventing you from investing your talents the way you desire? How can you remove them so that you can establish good works (in partnership with Holy Spirit) to the benefit of future generations and to the glory of God?

PRAYER

Father, build me up. Do not pull me down. Help me to stand before you deeply rooted and grounded. Give me what I need to sow unto future generations. What is the hope and the future you have for them? How can I partner with you to achieve it? Lord, identify stumbling blocks within me. I have counted the cost of separation from those things that are not pleasing to you and it is worth the price I must pay. Complete your work in me. Lord, as your scribe write on me and I will write what you have placed in me. In Jesus name, I pray, amen.

JONATHAN THE SCRIBE
Jehovah has given

Also Jonathan David's uncle was a counseller, a wise man, and a scribe: and Jehiel the son of Hachmoni was with the king's sons:

1 Chronicles 27:32

Week 4

The heaven, even the heavens, are the LORD'S: but the earth hath he given to the children of **men**.

Psalm 115:16, emphasis added

The word **men** means so much more than mere men! The root meaning is to be red, dyed red, as in to be reddened. This is to be washed in the blood of Jesus. The blood of Jesus makes us white as it takes away our sins and reconciles us back to God. Woven into the fabric of Psalm 115:16 is God truest intent. He gave the earth to the reddened children of men. Those that take after his Son. Those that are willing to go through the process of being reddened (Exodus 25:5).

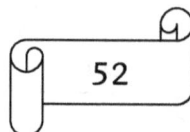

Evil men occupy the earth, but they will not get the eternal inheritance. The earth is in transition. It is the school through which the sons of God are learning to develop and walk in His nature. Among the evil men, we strengthen our love. Among the wicked, we grow in patience. Among the unbelieving, we learn how to share our testimony. Under attack, we learn how to fight and take authority.

As scribes, we share the lessons we learned. We record it for future generations to learn from and to be encouraged. What we do now will help us enter the new earth. What we do now will ensure that we are eternally in the presence of our God if we do well.

WEEK 4

Are you ready to produce more for the kingdom of God? What steps are you willing to take in order to increase for the Lord?

PRAYER

Lord, thank you! Thank you for the opportunity to learn from you. To be sharpened by you. To grow in you. Thank you for the tests that keep me alert and on my toes. Lord, examine me. What else do I need? Supply it according to your word. You supply all my needs according to your riches in glory through Christ Jesus.

Redden me. Make me like the skin of the ram soaked in the blood of Jesus. As Abel's blood cried out for him to you. Blood of Jesus cry out for me. Mercy, grace, forgiveness, love, hope, peace, endurance, encouragement, and cry out with what I need. Let my life be a beacon of hope for the lost so that they can find their way to your shore. Let nothing darken my light. I bind darkness and greater darkness. Let there be light in my inward parts that radiates and permeates the dark. Let it pierce the eyes of on lookers. Let it pierce their hearts to the glory of God in Jesus name, amen.

March

SHEVA THE SCRIBE
Jehovah Contends

And Sheva was scribe: and Zadok
and Abiathar were the priests:

2 Samuel 20:25

But thus saith the LORD, Even the
captives of the mighty shall be
taken away, and the prey of the
terrible shall be delivered: for I will
contend with him that contendeth
with thee, and I will save thy
children.

Isaiah 49:25

What a powerful thing it is when God contends for us! As scribes of the Lord, we can be confident that our God will oppose the forces of darkness on our behalf; however, he will not do it if we do not show up on the battlefield.

Many scribes suffer with intimidation. The spirit of fear lurks behind each word as the spirit of rejection waits to pounce with each submission. Worry and anxiety seem to be constant

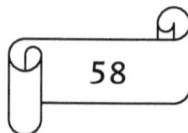

companions that murmur and whisper in our ears as they attempt to discourage us from perusing the course of God.

As scribes, we will experience setbacks. We will be rejected. People may even say negative things about our writing. Whatever is said is not to stop us from progressing along the path that the Lord has fashioned for us in Jesus name!

When we fall, we are to get back up.

For a just man falleth seven times, and riseth up again: but the wicked shall fall into mischief.

Proverbs 24:16

If we refuse to stand our ground before the enemy, we have given the battle to him, conceding that darkness has more power than light. If you are at that point of giving up as a scribe of the Lord, please don't. Ask for help. God is able to keep you from abandoning your post or succumbing to the wounds of the enemy.

A Psalm of David. Plead my cause,
O LORD, with them that strive
with me: fight against them that
fight against me.

Psalm 35:1

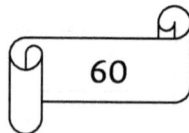

SHEVA THE SCRIBE
Jehovah Contends

And Sheva was scribe: and Zadok
and Abiathar were the priests:

2 Samuel 20:25

Week 1

But thus saith the LORD, Even the
captives of the mighty shall be
taken away, and the prey of the
terrible shall be delivered: for I will
contend with him that contendeth
with thee, and I will save thy
children.

Isaiah 49:25

So often, we may feel like captives. We may feel unable to move forward because something has its grips on us, holding us in place. It could be fear, lack of resources, or lack of an opportunity. Whatever it is specifically, we are confined to a place and our choices may appear limited. This is what it means to be a captive and to live in captivity.

The root meaning of *captive* is precious stone, a flame, fragments, or splinters. It means to break up. What is interesting is that the captives in Isaiah 49:25 were precious stones or flames of God. However, the enemy broke them up. He fragmented them and turned them into splinters or pieces. How often has setbacks or experiences shattered your heart? Or caused you to feel broken and hopeless? As a scribe, you are a precious stone unto the Lord. You are his burning flame. A light placed on a hill. How can you get your flame burning again? How can you cause it to burn brightly for the Lord?

WEEK 1

What things are you battling concerning your writing? What opportunities do you see for growth and expansion? For reclaiming territory?

PRAYER

Father, in the name of Jesus, open my eyes so that I can see. Enlarge my understanding so I can identify the areas in which I have become a captive of the enemy. Christ came to set me free. I desire to live a life of freedom in Christ Jesus help me to do so in every area of my life. I dedicate my hands and my being to you. Teach me how to contend for that which you have paid the price for me, in Jesus name, amen.

SHEVA THE SCRIBE
Jehovah Contends

And Sheva was scribe: and Zadok
and Abiathar were the priests:

2 Samuel 20:25

Week 2

But thus saith the LORD, Even the
captives of the mighty shall be
taken away, and the prey of the
terrible shall be delivered: for I will
contend with him that contendeth
with thee, and I will save thy
children.

Isaiah 49:25

In life, we often are in situations where another has the power to make decision concerning certain outcomes in our lives. We are in a sense, beholden to them. At times that can make us feel powerless or weak. It may seem as if we are not in control of our lives. The emotions that it could evoke can range from anger to complacency.

What do the words of Isaiah 49:15 speak to you?
How could the promise in the verse aid you as you
deal with your situation? What does it inspire?
Encourage? Kindle?

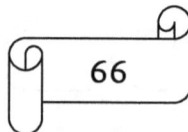

WEEK 2

What do you want God to do for you? When you consider the promise of Isaiah 49:15, how does it impact your point of view? How does it change the way you view yourself, the world, or others?

Father, in the name of Jesus, forgive me for looking at myself (**state how you looked at yourself**). Help me to see myself the way that you see me. Show me every area of captivity and teach me how to live a life of abundance. Every false thought I tear down and I ask that you teach me how to think as you do. I desire life, freedom, and fullness through Jesus. Help me, amen.

SHEVA THE SCRIBE
Jehovah Contends

And Sheva was scribe: and Zadok
and Abiathar were the priests:

2 Samuel 20:25

Week 3

But thus saith the LORD, Even the
captives of the mighty shall be
taken away, and the prey of the
terrible shall be delivered: for I will
contend with him that contendeth
with thee, and I will save thy
children.

Isaiah 49:25

Whether you know it or not you have an opponent who is always fighting against you. He does not want you to succeed in life and especially not in your work for Christ! He is your adversary. He is a contender for all that God has given you. He wants it. He yearns to take it from you (1 Peter 5:8).

Your adversary will use anything and anyone in order to gain ground against you. He will quarrel, complain, physically hinder you, strive against you, take legal action, and try to sue you in the court of heaven.

Despite this, you have an advocate (1 John 2:1, Lamentations 3:58-66)). He is willing and able to bring your case before the Father. He is skilled in how to present a defense against every word of the Devil. What has he said about you lately? Which part of what he has said have you believed? What do you intend to do about believing words whispered to you by the Devil?

WEEK 3

What steps will you take to *devastate* the enemy of your writing? How will you *tear down* his falsehood?

PRAYER

L ord of light and glory expose to me the lies that I have believed from the enemy. Help me to discern his voice from my own. Help me to recognize when he is hissing his foul and destructive words to me. Lord, teach me how to pull down every thought into captivity. Help me to me to make them obedient to Christ.

Casting down imaginations, and every high thing that exalteth itself against the knowledge of God, and bringing into captivity every thought to the obedience of Christ;

2 Corinthians 10:5

SHEVA THE SCRIBE
Jehovah Contends

And Sheva was scribe: and Zadok
and Abiathar were the priests:

2 Samuel 20:25

Week 4

But thus saith the LORD, Even the
captives of the mighty shall be
taken away, and the prey of the
terrible shall be delivered: for I will
contend with him that contendeth
with thee, and I will save thy
children.

Isaiah 49:25

D id you read the last part of Isaiah 49:25? "For I will contend with him that contendeth with thee, and I will save thy children." Let that soak in for a minute. What does that mean to you? How does that apply to your situation? What does that do to you emotionally?

Jehovah is going to contend with your enemy on your behalf! He is going to deliver you and save your children. What an assurance. What a wonderful promise.

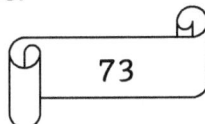

What are the things that you would like to ask
God to contend with for you? From whom would
you like him to save your children? What areas do
you need deliverance?

WEEK 4

T his week you are to take over territory. Uproot foul thoughts, silence lying tongues, and lay waste to the schemes of the enemy in your life. Write out what will be established in your life by the grace of God.

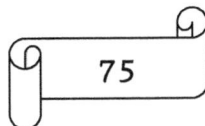

PRAYER

How would you pray to the Lord about all that you have shared above? Put it into words and lift it up to him. Let it be established by faith. Jehovah is your God and He is contending for you. He will teach you how to contend with the enemy. Believe and receive from him what you need to turn the tables on your opponent, your adversary in the name of Jesus, amen.

April

JEIEL THE SCRIBE
God Sweeps Away

Moreover Uzziah had an host of
fighting men, that went out to war
by bands, according to the number
of their account by the hand of
Jeiel the scribe and Maaseiah the
ruler, under the hand of Hananiah,
one of the king's captains.

2 Chronicles 26:11

I will utterly consume all things
from off the land, saith the LORD.

Zephaniah 1:2

The reign of Uzziah is a lesson for all who are appointed to positions of influence. Therefore, Uzziah's life is a lesson for every scribe. Uzziah began to rule in the place of his father, Amaziah, at the age of sixteen. He was from a prosperous spiritual lineage for his mother's name was *Jecoliah* or *Jecholiah* that meant, "Jehovah is able". While his father's name meant "Jehovah is mighty".

> And he sought God in the days of
> Zechariah, who had
> understanding in the visions of
> God: and as long as he sought the
> Lord, God made him to prosper.
>
> 2 Chronicles 26:5

Woven into his parents' name was an assurance of God's ability to do and act on Uzziah's behalf. It was part of his inheritance and birthright. Their names reminded Uzziah that God was strong, brave, bold, and solid. That he was able to overcome and prevail *over all enemies* for he was the one true God. It spoke to the fact that God could be trusted and depended on in times of battle or crisis.

Uzziah understood that to rule with success and prosperity he needed to rightly align himself with God. As a reward for his faithfulness to God, he was *marvelously* helped.

And he made in Jerusalem engines, invented by cunning men, to be on the towers and upon the bulwarks, to shoot arrows and great stones withal. And his name spread far abroad; for he was marvellously helped, till he was strong.

2 Corinthians 26:15

However, Uzziah did not remain dependent on God. *He started to rely and believe in his own abilities rather than God.* His heart became lofty, haughty, and arrogant. This brought about his own destruction (2 Chronicles 26:11-18). He went into the temple of the Lord and burnt incense upon the altar. The priests opposed him reminding him of the law of God. Uzziah did not accept the correction that was given to him. He became enraged with the priest. Leprosy rose up on his forehead in the house of God and in the presence of the priest. He remained a leper until his death.

But when he was strong, his heart
was lifted up to his destruction: for
he transgressed against the Lord
his God, and went into the temple
of the Lord to burn incense upon
the altar of incense.

2 Chronicles 26:16

If Uzziah had continued walking properly with
the Lord, Jehovah would have *Jeiel* all his enemies.
Jeiel means, "God sweeps away." As Uzziah
sought the Lord, he fulfilled his promise to him.
God removed his enemies from his path.

I will utterly consume all things
from off the land, saith the LORD.

Zephaniah 1:2

JEIEL THE SCRIBE
God Sweeps Away

Moreover Uzziah had an host of
fighting men, that went out to war
by bands, according to the number
of their account by the hand of
Jeiel the scribe and Maaseiah the
ruler, under the hand of Hananiah,
one of the king's captains.

2 Chronicles 26:11

Week 1

I will utterly consume all things
from off the land, saith the LORD.

Zephaniah 1:2

What does "God sweeps away" mean? It almost sounds as if God takes a giant broom and begins to do major house cleaning! That is what **Jeiel** means. He gathers them up and sweeps them together. Woven into the root meaning for **Jeiel** is the fact that God is, a mighty one, one possessing extraordinary strength and power, the one who sweeps His enemies together and removes them.

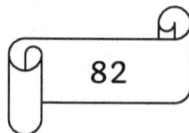

> I will utterly consume all things
> from off the land, saith the LORD.
>
> Zephaniah 1:2

When we explore the root meaning of the word **Jeiel**, we discover that it means to be a ram (sacrifice, food, skin that is dyed, for the tabernacle), a doorpost, a chief, strong man, leader or a mighty tree). The base meaning is to be a wealthy man, a noble, a person of prominence, and to be strong. In the negative sense, it is to be contemptuous with a belly or in one's body.

What does this indicate? As scribes, *we have great potential.* We can influence others to be more in Christ Jesus or less. We too can be *mighty scribes* for the Lord or we can be contemptuous scribes. God has given us eternal opportunity but we alone determine how we will use it. If we use it to the glory of God, we will demonstrate strength in how we twist the lies of the enemy. Meaning to bind it with truth so the light of Christ shines forth in all that we do.

According to 2 Chronicles 26:11, the official officer *Maaseiah* was in charge of the fighting men. The name *Masseiah* means "work of Jehovah". Therefore, it was clear that God intended to get full credit for the triumphs of the army. God was fashioning and shaping the earth in order to produce a *righteous harvest*. He was showing forth his strength as he twisted and formed it in order to bring forth his will.

As scribes of the Lord, we are also waging war for the kingdom of God. He has given us a seat of influence over the masses in order to fashion something that will produce fruitfulness for the kingdom. Therefore, we are to give him the credit for the work that he allows us to do in his name.

WEEK 1

Are there things that you have taken credit for rather than giving God the glory and acknowledgment for achieving them? If so, seize the opportunity today to make it right with God. The priest confronted Uzziah, but he did not recognize the opportunity that was given to him. He chose to become enraged instead.

PRAYER

Father, forgive me for taking credit for what you did. Lord, help me to give you the honor and glory for the works that you do. Help me to praise you for what you cause me to accomplish. All that I have, all I do is because of your gracious love toward me. Father, thank you. In Jesus name, amen.

JEIEL THE SCRIBE
God Sweeps Away

Moreover Uzziah had an host of
fighting men, that went out to war
by bands, according to the number
of their account by the hand of
Jeiel the scribe and Maaseiah the
ruler, under the hand of Hananiah,
one of the king's captains.

2 Chronicles 26:11

Week 2

I will utterly consume all things
from off the land, saith the LORD.

Zephaniah 1:2

Maaseiah was under the command of
Hananiah one of the king's captains. The
name **Hananiah** means, "God has
favored". God had surrounded Uzziah with his
favor. He showed him pity and mercy. In essence,
the Lord had bent down toward Uzziah in order to
give him aid to rule. God encamped round about
him as a covering.

As the scribes of the Lord, Jehovah is our covering. He has anointed us with the ability to pen words that will make a difference in the lives of others. He has charged us with a solemn responsibility that can only be achieved if we remain in him.

Has your heart become lifted up? Have you begun to write with formulas rather than being led by the spirit of God? Has that caused you to act presumptuously? Have you ignored the warning of those whom the Lord sent to correct your wayward decent?

Take time this week to seek Holy Spirit in the matter so that you do not become a spiritual leper before the Lord.

PRAYER

Heavenly Father you show favor on your children. Father favor me. Please help me to sweep away those things in my emotions, thoughts and behaviors that would derail me and cause me to be a leprous scribe. Give me ears that hear your correction. Give me the strength and determination so that I may do what is right even when it is not comfortable or it offends my sensitivities. Lord help me to look to you in all things. Forgive me where in I have stolen your glory, and enable me to give you credit for all things, for it is by your grace that I am able to do, in Jesus name I pray, amen.

JEIEL THE SCRIBE
God Sweeps Away

Moreover Uzziah had an host of
fighting men, that went out to war
by bands, according to the number
of their account by the hand of
Jeiel the scribe and Maaseiah the
ruler, under the hand of Hananiah,
one of the king's captains.

2 Chronicles 26:11

Week 3

I will utterly consume all things
from off the land, saith the LORD.

Zephaniah 1:2

One of **Jeiel's** duties was to be the secretary of the King. He was both a narrator and historical recorder cataloging all acts of the king's *irregular predatory warriors.*

King Uzziah had warriors who did **exploits**. They were the mighty men. They employed tactics that required stealth, cunning, and skill.

And such as do wickedly against
the covenant shall he corrupt by
flatteries: but the people that do
know their God shall be strong,
and do exploits.

Daniel 11:32

Because these mighty heroes, god-like men knew their God they were able to do great exploits (2 Chronicles 26:12). The word **exploit** means to do anything. These warriors were able to do anything and be successful. They operated in an unorthodox fashion, but it was profitable because God was with them.

Uzziah's sin was that he allowed pride to usurp his heart. He took pride in numbers, weapons, and the skills of men. Pride went before his fall.

Pride goes before destruction, and
a haughty spirit before a fall.

Proverbs 16:18

Each of us has a duty to the Lord to represent his character and nature in all that we do. It is not a role that we play in life, but rather the nature of Christ that is made evident through us. Christ called us to life therefore; anything that would prevent us from achieving that mandate should be discarded. Take time this week to ask the Lord to identify any areas *of pride* or *haughtiness*. There is still time to cleanse yourself unto the Lord.

WEEK 3

What can you do knowing that God is with you?

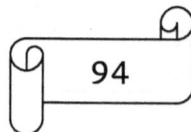

PRAYER

Lord search me and know me. If there is any secret sin, remove it from me. I break my agreement with it and I let it go. Lord, cut it off from me so that it no longer has a hold on me. Place a dividing line between it and me. As the heavens are far from the earth, so to make this sin far from me in the name of Jesus.

Lord, help me to place my confidence in you and not in my skills, formulas or in others. Help me to be focused. I desire to be as erect and immovable as a pillar that supports a building, as a palm tree that is straight with arms lifted in praise and thanksgiving before God. Thank you Jehovah, amen.

JEIEL THE SCRIBE
God Sweeps Away

Moreover Uzziah had an host of
fighting men, that went out to war
by bands, according to the number
of their account by the hand of
Jeiel the scribe and Maaseiah the
ruler, under the hand of Hananiah,
one of the king's captains.

2 Chronicles 26:11

Week 4

I will utterly consume all things
from off the land, saith the LORD.

Zephaniah 1:2

Under the watchful eye of the prophet Zechariah, Uzziah prospered because he sought God. The name **Zechariah** means, "Jehovah remembers." As Uzziah sought the Lord, Jehovah remembered his promises to him. With each occurrence of seeking God, it prompted God to recall his duty to favor Uzziah with his strength, ability, and faithfulness. It reminded Jehovah of the work that he was to complete.

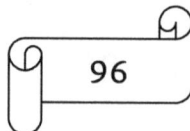

Seeking the Scribes Anointing

God has begun a work in each of us and he is faithful to complete it (Philippians 1:6). However, we have a duty to seek him at all times (Psalm 34). We can make the same choice as Uzziah and place our trust in publishers, the New York Times Best Sellers list, marketing strategies, writing formulas, or the opinions of men or we can place our trust in the Lord our God believing that he will prosper us as we write for the kingdom of heaven.

Some trust in chariots, and some in horses: but we will remember the name of the LORD our God.

Psalm 20:7

WEEK 4

What will you choose to do? Share your plan write it out and make it plain (Habakkuk 2:2).

PRAYER

As you view your plan, what would you like God to do? What would you like him to do for you? What would you like him to do in you? When you are ready write out your prayer here and date it so that it will be a remembrance for you and your house.

May

ELISHAMA THE SCRIBE
My God has Heard

And they went in to the king into the court, but they laid up the roll in the chamber of Elishama the scribe, and told all the words in the ears of the king.

Jeremiah 36:20

I cried unto him with my mouth, and he was extolled with my tongue.

If I regard iniquity in my heart, the Lord will not hear me:

But verily God hath heard me; he hath attended to the voice of my prayer.

Psalm 66:17-19

Jeremiah 36 recounts an interesting time in the history of Israel. It chronicles the lengths that God went to in order to encourage his people to return to him. Jeremiah dictated the message from the Lord to Baruch. *Jeremiah's* name meant, "Whom Jehovah has appointed." *Baruch's* name meant, "Blessed." From this, we can deduce that the message that was given to Jeremiah from God was appointed to bring about a blessing to those who heard and responded correctly to the message.

Jeremiah hoped that when the people heard the message that they would repent to the Lord (Jeremiah 36:7). When the word was read, in the house of the Lord, a fast was proclaimed (Jeremiah 36:8). Baruch continued to read the word of the Lord in the chambers of the higher court in the Lord's house (Jeremiah 36:10). As the serious nature of the word spread, Baruch read it in the chamber of the scribe's within the king's house. Those who heard the word of the Lord were filled with fear and acted to bring the matter to the attention of the king.

Jehudi read three or four pages from the message. King Jehoiakim nor his servants were filled with fear at the reading of the sacred word of the Lord. They did not rend their clothing or kneel in repentance before God. Jehudi *treated the scroll with contempt; he cut it with a penknife, and cast pieces into the fire.* Elnathan, Delaiah, and Gemariah rulers of Judah requested that the King refrain from burning the scroll but he refused to listen to them.

The scribes and princes who had heard the word read in the scribe's chamber had originally responded with fear to the message of God. They commanded Baruch to hide himself along with

Jeremiah letting no one know where they were hidden. They knew that once the message was delivered in the chamber of the king the lives of both Jeremiah and Baruch would be in jeopardy (Jeremiah 36:19).

In the presence of the king, the princes did not follow through with their convictions. They did not counsel the king to repent. They did not suggest he take the word of the Lord seriously. They did not warn King Jehoiakim not to touch the anointed of God. They remained quiet in order to preserve their own safety and self-interests. The king sent men to locate Baruch and Jeremiah, but the Lord had hid them.

But the king commanded
Jerahmeel the son of Hammelech,
and Seraiah the son of Azriel, and
Shelemiah the son of Abdeel, to
take Baruch the scribe and
Jeremiah the prophet: but the
LORD hid them."

Jeremiah 36:26

Kingdom Scribes
Seeking the Scribes Anointing
ELISHAMA THE SCRIBE
My God has Heard

"Then he went down into the
king's house, into the scribe's
chamber: and, lo, all the princes
sat there, even Elishama the scribe,
and Delaiah the son of Shemaiah,
and Elnathan the son of Achbor,
and Gemariah the son of Shaphan,
and Zedekiah the son of Hananiah,
and all the princes."

Jeremiah 36:12

Week 1

---

unto him with my mouth, and he
was extolled with my tongue.

If I regard iniquity in my heart, the
Lord will not hear me:

But verily God hath heard me; he
hath attended to the voice of my
prayer.

Psalm 66:17-19

Assembled in the scribe's chamber was an impressive cast of princes, rulers, and noble men. Each one carried a name that represented an aspect of Gods ability. **Elishama** represented God's ability to hear for his name meant, **"My God has heard."** Delaiah, the son of Shemaiah, represented Jehovah ability to be brought low to hear his people for his name meant **"Jehovah has drawn"** is distressed, or brought low. While his father's name Shemaiah meant, **"Heard by Jehovah"** or to listen.

Elnathan's name meant, **"God has given."** While his father's name Achbor meant, mouse (as in the sense of attacking, nibbling), a spider (sense of entangling). Elnathan had the ability to be a mighty representative for God, yet at his base, he had the inheritance of a mouse one who attacks though nibbling. He lived up to his natural lineage when he slew the prophet Urijah (Uriah), which means, **"Jehovah is my light"** or **"Yahweh is my flame."**

As scribes of Jehovah, we may possess great potential to expose the world to the goodness of God, but the manifestation of that reality hinges on how deep our convictions are in the Lord. Each of these men had an opportunity to sow righteousness as rulers yet they were shortsighted. They did not uphold the righteous standard of God. Instead, they allowed themselves to support an ungodly king. In spite of God knowing where their true allegiance lay, he gave them another opportunity to live up to the call that was placed on them by their given name.

WEEK 1

How well are you living up to the call that has been placed on you? How are you representing Christ to those around you without corruption? In what areas can you improve? What is your plan? When will you begin?

PRAYER

L ord, in the name of Jesus, please surround me with those who will be true to the call you have placed on their lives. Give me true friends with a heart for God and a steadfast dedication. Lord, help us to support and encourage one another in truth and spirit. Father, cut off any relationships that would pull me away from you or cause my walk to be corrupted in the name of Jesus, amen.

Elishama the Scribe
My God has Heard

"Then he went down into the king's house, into the scribe's chamber: and, lo, all the princes sat there, even Elishama the scribe, and Delaiah the son of Shemaiah, and Elnathan the son of Achbor, and Gemariah the son of Shaphan, and Zedekiah the son of Hananiah, and all the princes."

Jeremiah 36:12

Week 2

---

unto him with my mouth, and he was extolled with my tongue.

If I regard iniquity in my heart, the Lord will not hear me:

But verily God hath heard me; he hath attended to the voice of my prayer.

Psalm 66:17-19

Present in the scribe's chamber was Gemariah whose name meant, **"Jehovah has accomplished."** It speaks of God's ability to complete or end something. It resonates with the assurance that God is able to perfect, perform, and cause things to cease or come to an end. His father's name Shaphan means **rock badger**. The core meaning of his name is to hide, cover over, or conceal treasure. It almost denotes God's ability to cover or hide his riches. As in how God protected the prophet Jeremiah from the hand of the king that wished to slay him.

It may also represent God's ability to expose the hidden treasures of the enemy. God has the ability to see all; therefore, he alone is able to see where things are hidden. As he alone is able to hide that which he does not want discovered.

And I will give thee the treasures of darkness, and hidden riches of secret places, that thou mayest know that I, the LORD, which call thee by thy name, am the God of Israel.

Isaiah 45:3

Unfortunately, for Gemariah, he did not allow God to accomplish all that he could have through him for he did not stand up for righteousness. He allowed his witness to be tarnished and nullified. He did not respond in shame, grief, or despair when he heard the word of Jehovah read in the presence of the king. As a part of the King's

Counsel, he did not admonish him to heed the word of the Lord.

As anointed scribes of the Lord, Jehovah has placed things in us that he alone is able to bring out. He also knows the things that the enemy has confiscated that rightly belongs to those who are called to the service of the King.

> A Psalm of David. The earth is the LORD'S, and the fulness thereof; the world, and they that dwell therein.
>
> Psalm 24:1

All belongs to the Lord therefore, he alone has the right to hide it or dispense of it as he sees fit. In order to be righteous witnesses for the Lord, we have to allow him to accomplish and complete the work that he has started. We have to allow him to do as he wills with our lives so that his untarnished glory will manifest in us and through our writings.

WEEK 2

What treasures do you desire to have recovered from the hand of the enemy? Do you desire that God will reveal the hidden treasures within you?

PRAYER

Father, I ask in the name of Jesus that you forgive me for not guarding the treasures that you placed in my hands. The treasures that I did not value and took for granted. I ask that you restore them unto me. Lord, teach me how to grow in them and use them to your names honor and glory. Help me not to despise the gifts and talents you have given me, but rather to value them, sowing them wherever I can, trusting and believing in you for the increase.

Lord, there are things, which you have hidden in me. Things that are designed for your glory. Please Lord, unearth them. Expose them to the light so that I may see, know and understand. Spirit of God help me. Sow life and fruitfulness. Sow glory and honor. Lord teach me to handle them with care and respect. You are the giver of all good gifts help me to treat them and honor them with goodness for in so doing I honor you. Thank you Jesus for hearing in your name amen.

ELISHAMA THE SCRIBE
My God has Heard

"Then he went down into the king's house, into the scribe's chamber: and, lo, all the princes sat there, even Elishama the scribe, and Delaiah the son of Shemaiah, and Elnathan the son of Achbor, and Gemariah the son of Shaphan, and Zedekiah the son of Hananiah, and all the princes."

Jeremiah 36:12

Week 3

---

unto him with my mouth, and he was extolled with my tongue.

If I regard iniquity in my heart, the Lord will not hear me:

But verily God hath heard me; he hath attended to the voice of my prayer.

Psalm 66:17-19

Jehovah is righteous. Zedekiah's name was a reminder that **God is indeed righteous**. As such, he is to be revered and treated with reverence. Jehovah is rightness, justice, ethical

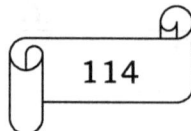

rightness, justness in weights and measures, and righteous in administration of government.

Zedekiah's father's name Hananiah means, **"God has favored."** It is God's ability to have pity or mercy on people. It reveals that, although Jehovah is righteous in all things, he has the capacity to show compassion to the inhabitants of the earth.

The noble men that gathered in the scribe's chamber had all they needed to operate with spiritual righteousness. As they called one another's name, they lifted the standards and responsibility to which they were called. They had a fiduciary duty to lead the people in the righteousness of God. Yet he did not.

Although we are told in Jeremiah 36:9 that a fast was proclaimed in the fifth year of Jehoiakim's reign. It was merely for show for the king allowed the prophetic word of the Lord to be burnt. He dispatched men to apprehend Jeremiah and Baruch and the noble men of Judah remained silent.

WEEK 3

As scribes, we are called to lead, oversee, and to be an official representative of the kingdom of God. We are to do it in a manner that will establish the righteousness of God at all times and in all seasons.

When it comes to your writing, have you remained silent when you should have spoken up? Were there things that you were to address that you failed to do due to fear, intimidation, or self-interest? What do you intend to do now?

PRAYER

Establish me, oh Lord, as your scribe in the earth. Make me firm and immovable. Help me to write for you, speak up, and to affirm with all that I do that you are Lord. Father, help me not to be silenced by mobs or the pressures of groups. Help me to stand in truth and love. Let me be a magnet to truth seekers as I lift you up draw them according to your word, in Jesus name amen.

ELISHAMA THE SCRIBE
My God has Heard

"Then he went down into the
king's house, into the scribe's
chamber: and, lo, all the princes
sat there, even Elishama the scribe,
and Delaiah the son of Shemaiah,
and Elnathan the son of Achbor,
and Gemariah the son of Shaphan,
and Zedekiah the son of Hananiah,
and all the princes."

Jeremiah 36:12

Week 4

---

unto him with my mouth, and he
was extolled with my tongue.

If I regard iniquity in my heart, the
Lord will not hear me:

But verily God hath heard me; he
hath attended to the voice of my
prayer.

Psalm 66:17-19

Jeremiah 36 demonstrates *how easy it is to become corrupted.* Although God has a mighty call on the lives of his children, each one of us has to make the decision to establish and uphold his untarnished nature in circumstances and ourselves. At times, it may be challenging to do so for it could put our lives at risk or cause us to fall out of favor with men.

What is evident here is that God has a hope and a future for each of us. One to which we are called to fulfill. However, in order for it to be fulfilled, we need to obey *his word and respond properly to his correction.* Although we can pretend to be on the Lord's side, inevitably something will come along which will **force us to declare or demonstrate our true allegiance.** Many in Jeremiah's day sided with the king. The few stood for the righteousness of the Lord.

If our allegiance is for another, we have time to correct it. If our loyalty is to a group or to our craft, we have time to make the necessary adjustments. As scribe's of the Lord, let us not allow anything to corrupt the call that God has placed on our lives.

In which areas have you allowed your call to be corrupted? What are you willing to do about it? How can you establish your commitment to God? What are you willing to do right now to start the process?

PRAYER

Speak to the Lord. Pour out your heart to him. Share with him what you have done, how you feel about it (repent), and what you intend to do from this day forward.

June

EZRA THE SCRIBE
Help

This Ezra went up from Babylon;
and he was a ready scribe in the
law of Moses, which the LORD God
of Israel had given: and the king
granted him all his request,
according to the hand of the LORD
his God upon him.

Ezra 7:6

For Ezra had prepared his heart to
seek the law of the LORD, and to do
it, and to teach in Israel statutes
and judgments.

Ezra 7:10

The name **Ezra** means **help**. Its core meaning comes from the word *ezrah*, which means one who helps, gives assistance, or one who supports in times of distress and hardship (succor). The base meaning of ezrah comes from the word 'ezer which also means help, succor, or one who helps.

The first use of the word Ezer was in Genesis 2:18 when God spoke and said that it was not good for man to be alone and he would make him a helpmate. The helpmate that God made for Adam denotes the role and function of one who is of assistance to another. This is the role that Ezra had in the plan of God.

Ezra was a priest and a scribe. He was instrumental in the rebuilding of the Jerusalem Temple. He also took it upon himself to prepare himself in the law of the Lord in order to teach Israel the judgments and statutes of God.

EZRA THE SCRIBE
Help

---

*This Ezra went up from Babylon;
and he was a ready scribe in the
law of Moses, which the LORD God
of Israel had given: and the king
granted him all his request,
according to the hand of the LORD
his God upon him.*

Ezra 7:6

Week 1

---

*For Ezra had prepared his heart to
seek the law of the LORD, and to do
it, and to teach in Israel statutes
and judgments.*

Ezra 7:10

The Lord is constantly looking throughout the earth for people to whom he can assign work to do. Occasionally he found such men who were willing to assist God in carrying out his purpose (Nehemiah 3). At other times he could find no one which resulted in God's indignation being poured out and the consuming fire of the Lord spewing forth on the heads of people (Ezekiel 22:30-31).

Kingdom Scribes
Seeking the Scribes Anointing

As in times past, the Lord is looking for individuals who are willing to stand in the gap not only as priests, but also as scribes. A priest of Jehovah is one who undertakes the cause of the Lord and is willing to intercede between God and men.

> But ye are a chosen generation, a royal priesthood, an holy nation, a peculiar people; that ye should shew forth the praises of him who hath called you out of darkness into his marvellous light:
>
> *1 Peter 2:9*

WEEK 1

Are you willing to stand in the gap as a priest of the Lord? How can you fulfill this role as priest as you write for the Lord as his scribe?

PRAYER

As you ponder the questions above, what do you believe you need from God to fulfill his purpose? What things do you need to be increased?

Ye lust, and have not: ye kill, and desire to have, and cannot obtain: ye fight and war, yet ye have not, because ye ask not.

3 Ye ask, and receive not, because ye ask amiss, that ye may consume it upon your lusts.

James 4:2-3

How does James 4:2-3, impact your prayers? In light of the impact, what will you adjust, do or eliminate?

Write your prayer here (date it) so that you will remember what you asked God for on this day in Jesus name, amen.

EZRA THE SCRIBE
Help

This Ezra went up from Babylon;
and he was a ready scribe in the
law of Moses, which the LORD God
of Israel had given: and the king
granted him all his request,
according to the hand of the LORD
his God upon him.

Ezra 7:6

Week 2

For Ezra had prepared his heart to
seek the law of the LORD, and to do
it, and to teach in Israel statutes
and judgments.

Ezra 7:10

As scribes, we are employed to as recorders or keepers of records for the Lord even if it's just for our own family. We can record our testimony, experiences, prayers, areas where God has delivered us, or revelations that the Lord has given us thus, establishing a written testament of what God has done and who God has proven himself to be on our behalf.

Are you willing to be of assistance to the cause of Christ through the publication of your testimony? Are you willing to share it with future generations? How could this act have a significant impact on your family and others?

PRAYER

Lord help me to live a life of significance. Sowing the meaning of life in all that I do. Help me to seize the opportunities that you gave in order to bring glory to your name and not my own. Lord, I desire to be trustworthy to the cause of Christ. Root out anything that would hinder or derail me from achieving your purpose for my life. Make me a true and powerful witness for Christ. One that stands firm and is guided by your spirit I pray, amen.

EZRA THE SCRIBE
Help

---

*This Ezra went up from Babylon;
and he was a ready scribe in the
law of Moses, which the LORD God
of Israel had given: and the king
granted him all his request,
according to the hand of the LORD
his God upon him.*

Ezra 7:6

Week 3

---

*For Ezra had prepared his heart to
seek the law of the LORD, and to do
it, and to teach in Israel statutes
and judgments.*

Ezra 7:10

Ezra the scribe has given us a wonderful example of how we are to serve the Lord. First, we are to *prepare our heart to seek God*. What did he do? He fixed his heart; he determined to enquire of the Lord. He frequently visited the law of God. This was a conscientious choice. It is not something that he stumbled into!

The heart of a man is not naturally inclined to seek the things of God. It must be trained to do so.

Ezra understood this that is why he visited the law frequently. He washed his mind in the word of God.

Secondly, we must force our hearts to do what we discover. This indicates that we must exercise authority over our heart compelling it to do what it does not want to do. To **"do it"** (Ezra 7:10) is to fashion or make something. It is to put in order or produce a thing. Therefore, it is clear that Ezra's actions was creating something as God created the firmament in Genesis 1:7. **'Asah** is the Hebrew word used to describe Ezra's activity and it is the same word that is used to denote God's making of the firmament in Genesis 1.

Ezra created his heart by applying the word of God regularly and consistently. He wanted to be of help to God and God in turn helped him.

Often we desire to share a message or want to teach others before we take time to learn the lesson for ourselves. Ezekiel outlines the proper procedure in order to be of assistance to the Lord (Ezekiel 3:1-4).

Moreover he said unto me, Son of
man, eat that thou findest; eat this
roll, and go speak unto the house
of Israel.

So I opened my mouth, and he
caused me to eat that roll.

And he said unto me, Son of man,
cause thy belly to eat, and fill thy
bowels with this roll that I give
thee. Then did I eat it; and it was in
my mouth as honey for sweetness.

Ezekiel 3:1-3

Before we can share or teach, we are to take time
to seek, study, and learn. We are to go through the
process of being made new from the inside out. By
studying the word of the Lord, he was made
aware of God's standards. As he forced himself to
comply with God's word his heart was changed or
fashioned differently than it was before. His
stony heart was replaced and a heart of flesh was
given (Ezekiel 36:26).

What is the current state of your heart? What does it believe, desire or long for? How do these things line up with the word of God? If you are not sure, are you willing to invest the time to seek the Lord concerning it? Are you willing to do what it is he says? Are you an Ezra?

PRAYER

Lord, help me to eat what you teach. Help me to study what you provide. Help me to take the beam from my eye before I seek to correct others. Lord, help me to follow all the things that you teach so that they do not testify against me on the final day. Lord, your word is sweet help me to consume it daily and be generous to share it with others in the spirit of love to your glory I pray amen.

EZRA THE SCRIBE
Help

---

*This Ezra went up from Babylon;
and he was a ready scribe in the law
of Moses, which the LORD God of
Israel had given: and the king
granted him all his request,
according to the hand of the LORD
his God upon him.*

Ezra 7:6

Week 4

---

*For Ezra had prepared his heart to
seek the law of the LORD, and to do
it, and to teach in Israel statutes and
judgments.*

Ezra 7:10

The call placed on Ezra's life is similar to the call placed on the life of every believer. Christ commands us to obey his commandments. *It would be difficult to obey the commands of our Savior **if we do not know them!***

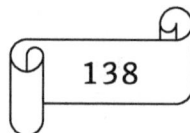

If ye love me, keep my
commandments.

John 14:15

How can we profess love for Jesus if we are not
willing to obey? Therefore, in order to establish
our love we must obey, and in order to obey we
must know what it is that we are to obey. This
intrinsic relationship highlights the wisdom of
Ezra's actions. For in order to be God's (Christ's)
helpers here on the earth we need to be rightly
positioned to be of assistance in time of hardship
or distress. When we know the word of the Lord,
we can speak a word in and out of season and it
will be a blessing to those who hear it.

The Lord GOD hath given me the
tongue of the learned, that I
should know how to speak a word
in season to him that is weary: he
wakeneth morning by morning, he
wakeneth mine ear to hear as the
learned.

Isaiah 50:4

**The truth is if we are unwilling to learn we are
unfit to teach.** Every *good* teacher must first be a
willing student.

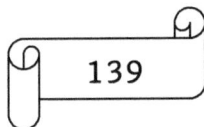

The root meaning of **Ezra** is to gird, or surround. It is to defend. Ezra was a defender of God and as such, he had to know God and know what God expected of him. The word gird is to fix, bind, restrain or tighten. Therefore, Ezra's role was as a mighty warrior of God. He fixed the word of God to himself as battle gear. He used it to restrain and bind the enemy (sin, temptations etc.) but he also used it as a way of tightening God's hold on the people so they would not fall prey to the enemy. When we defend God and the cause of God, he will surely give us the victory. As scribes we are to be ready to aid God in battle and be determined that, the victory must be the Lord's in Jesus name.

WEEK 4

Were there lessons that you were unwilling to learn in prior seasons? Are you willing to learn them now? What has changed? What has remained the same? Who are you in Christ? Who do you desire to be in him?

PRAYER

There are times when no one else can pray the prayer that you need. Only you can express your thoughts, feelings and desires unto the Lord. If you are not sure what to pray, ask Holy Spirit. He will help you and even pray for you. Trust him to do as he has promised.

May the Lord root you in faith and keep you by his love, in Jesus name amen.

July

SHIMSHAI THE SCRIBE
Sunny

Rehum the chancellor and
Shimshai the scribe wrote a letter
against Jerusalem to Artaxerxes
the king in this sort:

Ezra 4:8

For the LORD God is a sun and
shield: the LORD will give grace
and glory: no good thing will he
withhold from them that walk
uprightly.

Psalm 84:11

The scribe **Shimshai** was a Samaritan. Samaritans were considered half-breeds and were despised among the Jews. When the work to rebuild the temple of Lord began several of the inhabitants offered to work alongside the Jews to complete the task. Those in charge rejected their offer. As a result, several of these men wrote to King Artaxerxes against Jerusalem (Ezra 4).

Although Shimshai's name meant sunny and he was employed as the scribe for Rehum whose name means compassion or compassionate they did not live up to the meaning of their names. They were motivated by self-interested and were instrumental in working against the people of God.

As writers of the king, we are called to be bright and brilliant lights in the earth. We are to be candles set on a hill. Furthermore, we are to show compassion for those around us. Although these men offered to help the Jews rebuild, their true intent was to oppose the work and to exercise influence that was to their *selfish benefit*. In this matter, they operated like the **cockatrice** that cleaves close to a thing in order to split it asunder. Thankfully, the Jews were able to *discern* their true intent and prevented them from weaving a spider's web to entangle them or lay eggs of destruction for them to eat (Isaiah 59:5).

SHIMSHAI THE SCRIBE
Sunny

Rehum the chancellor and Shimshai the scribe wrote a letter against Jerusalem to Artaxerxes the king in this sort:

Ezra 4:8

Week 1

For the LORD God is a sun and shield: the LORD will give grace and glory: no good thing will he withhold from them that walk uprightly.

Psalm 84:11

Shimshai's name meant sunny however, he did not reflect the nature of his name. God on the other hand is called a sun and he is *sunny*. The root meaning for sun is brilliant as in brightness and splendor. It also means the glittering nature of a shield (how it shines).

God surrounds, covers and defends his people. He places a hedge of security around us. Have you encountered people like **Shimshai**? How did the experience make you feel? How does knowing that God is your sun and shield make you feel?

WEEK 1

Currently our souls are undergoing the process of sanctification through the power of God. We are challenged regularly to abandon wrong mindsets, emotions, and motivations. What are some of the items Holy Spirit is nudging you about? Are you willing to let them go? Are you willing to allow him to fashion you into a brilliant light for the King of kings?

Are there areas in your life where you have worked against the plan or the people of God, where you have been a Shimshai?

PRAYER

Jehovah you are my sun. You are brilliant and majestic, awesome and wholly beautiful. I ask that you cause me to be radiant, beautiful inside and out. Help me that your glory will cause me to be a light that can't be hidden. Father, strip away everything that is not like you. Every cloud of darkness that is dimming the light of Christ within me. Help me to live a life that transparently shows who Christ is and what he has done in the name of Jesus.

SHIMSHAI THE SCRIBE
Sunny

Rehum the chancellor and
Shimshai the scribe wrote a letter
against Jerusalem to Artaxerxes
the king in this sort:

Ezra 4:8

Week 2

---

*For the LORD God is a sun and
shield: the LORD will give grace and
glory: no good thing will he withhold
from them that walk uprightly.*

Psalm 84:11

The name **Rehum** means compassion. It is to have a tender affection or to deeply love another. As chancellor, he ruled over the area. Therefore, if we put the two names together we find that it should have been a bright place flowing with tender affection. This was not the case. However, God loved Jerusalem with tender compassion and they were in the light of his presence.

Although at times it may seem dark and dreary, we are constantly in the presence of God. We are in the light of his presence.

Arise, shine; for thy light is come, and the glory of the LORD is risen upon thee.

Isaiah 60:1

This then is the message, which we have heard of him, and declare unto you, that God is light, and in him is no darkness at all.

1 John 1:5

For by their own sword they did not possess the land, And their own arm did not save them, But Your right hand and Your arm and the light of Your presence, For You favored them.

Psalm 44:3

> While he was still speaking, a
> bright cloud overshadowed them,
> and behold, a voice out of the
> cloud said, "This is My beloved Son,
> with whom I am well-pleased;
> listen to Him!"
>
> Matthew 17:5

That knowledge should fill our hearts with hope and encouragement, for where we can see no way God has already lit a way of escape for us.

Compassion and light. As scribes of Jehovah, we are to be full of compassion and continually shedding light. At times, this can be challenging. How can we obtain it?

> Finally, be ye all of one mind,
> having compassion one of another,
> love as brethren, be pitiful, be
> courteous: Not rendering evil for
> evil, or railing for railing: but
> contrariwise blessing; knowing
> that ye are thereunto called, that
> ye should inherit a blessing.
>
> 1 Peter 3:8-9

By being of one mind. By allowing the mind of Christ to be in us (Philippian 2:5). We have to make the choice to let Jesus's mind reside in us. This is the only way we will be able to live with compassion for one another.

How are your motivations and actions? How well do you shed light and sow compassion?

PRAYER

Lord, help me to be a bright light wherever I am. Help me to sow seeds of tender love in the lives of others. Help me to live what I believe so that you are glorified in the name of Jesus. Increase your glory over my life and help me to pass it on to my descendants in Jesus name, amen.

SHIMSHAI THE SCRIBE
Sunny

Rehum the chancellor and
Shimshai the scribe wrote a letter
against Jerusalem to Artaxerxes
the king in this sort:

Ezra 4:8

Week 3

For the LORD God is a sun and
shield: the LORD will give grace and
glory: no good thing will he withhold
from them that walk uprightly.

Psalm 84:11

It is interesting that **Rehum** had nine companions that joined him in writing to the king. They were the Dinaites, Apharsathchites, Tarpelites, Apharsites, Archevites, Babylonians, Susanchites, Dehavites, and Elamites. These inhabitants populated Samaria. Each was opposed to the rebuilding of Jerusalem.

From their names, we know that the Dinaites represented *judgment.* The Apharsachites brought about division by *deception.* The Tarpelites were of *the fallen*. The Apharsites also caused *division*. The Archevites who were lengthy or long as in *stretching out, to make long, prolonging or to extend something.* The Babylonians *caused confusion by mixing.* The Susanchites (inhabitant of Shushan) meaning *lily, to exult, rejoice,* or *display joy.* The Dehavites *the sickly.* The Elamites that represents their *heaps.* At its root is *eternity and to conceal.* To be a dissembler or to hide oneself.

From this cast of characters we can see that the opposition against the returnees was fierce. This indicates that when the enemy comes against us he is willing to use every tactic at his disposal in order to break us in pieces.

According to E. W. Bullinger in his book **Number in Scripture** the number nine, represents judgment, finality, and the conclusion of a matter. Here we see that the enemy pronounced judgment on the project of God. However, God was in the midst and his judgment overrode the enemy.

When God is on our side who can stand against? Who can triumph over us? Whose word can supersede God? No one! Not men, evil spirits, spiritual wickedness, demons, principles, rulers or powers. No one! (Romans 8:38-39).

WEEK 3

The agents of darkness will attempt to attack our judgment. They will try to deceive us. They will send showers of confusion. Are there areas concerning your calling that you suspect the enemy has been at work? Are you ready to change that forever? What has God pronounced for you? Do you agree and believe what God has said? Are you ready to enforce the judgment of God on the enemy's opposition?

PRAYER

Write down your prayer of deliverance. It is a warfare prayer. Ask Holy Spirit to help you identify those things that are fighting against you. Remember we do not war against flesh and blood although they may use human beings to advance their plans. Your enemy is the same that tried to tempt Christ. Satan and his helpers are the ones behind the attacks and they are the ones that must be dislodged and stopped. Are you ready to release judgment?

SHIMSHAI THE SCRIBE
Sunny

Rehum the chancellor and
Shimshai the scribe wrote a letter
against Jerusalem to Artaxerxes
the king in this sort:

Ezra 4:8

Week 4

*For the LORD God is a sun and
shield: the LORD will give grace and
glory: no good thing will he withhold
from them that walk uprightly.*

Psalm 84:11

As we know Satan does not want us to progress in building the temple of God within us. He has thrown many diversionary things our way. In order to divide us from the purpose of God. He wants us to become like him the fallen. He aspires to extend his territory to include us. Therefore, he wages war against us and the messengers of God to prolong things (Daniel 10:13).

His aim is to rejoice over us. He wants to cloak us in darkness so that we will not know who we are in Christ and who we are called to be. He does this by hiding himself so that we do not *spiritual discern* that he is behind the opposition. If he succeeds, we will become spiritually malignant and sickly.

Our best weapon is to rely on the Lord and to cry out for discernment.

WEEK 4

Are you ready to ask Holy Spirit for help? Are there areas in your writing or life that you believe have succumbed to the attack of the enemy? Are you ready to oppose him and reclaim the territory for the Lord?

S pecifically list what has been confiscated by the enemy. Then write a prayer for **recovery**. If you have agreed with the enemy break the agreement and repent for coming into agreement with a lie.

August

Shebna the Scribe
Vigor

And when they had called to the
king, there came out to them
Eliakim the son of Hilkiah, which
was over the household, and
Shebna the scribe, and Joah the son
of Asaph the recorder.

2 Kings 18:18

For he shall grow up before him as
a tender plant, and as a root out of
a dry ground: he hath no form nor
comeliness; and when we shall see
him, there is no beauty that we
should desire him.

Isaiah 53:2

The scribe **Shebna** was the secretary of King Hezekiah. His name means "vigor" that comes from a root, which means to grow. According to the Gesenius' Hebrew-Chaldee Lexicon **Shebna** also means tender youth.

According to the Merriam –Webster Dictionary vigor means active bodily or mental strength or force. It is active healthy well-balanced growth especially of plants. It is force.

Shebna was a man who had grown in strength and force. He followed a path of development of his own choosing however, his progression was not healthy or rightly balanced.

Shebna was once in charge of the King's household until the prophet Isaiah delivered a word from the Lord concerning his fate (Isaiah 22:15-25). From the severity of God's judgment, it is evident that Shebna grew in the ways of the wicked. He was proud and deceitful. Shebna was told that the Lord was going to carry him away and another would take his place. Eliakim a servant of the Lord would be appointed to the esteemed position Shebna once had (Isaiah 22:20).

Shebna would have had no doubt as to whom was performing the work of **Eliakim's** elevation for **Eliakim's** name means "God rises" or "God sets up". Therefore, if Shebna had any issue with the word that Isaiah gave him he would have had to address it directly with God!

The difference between Eliakim and Shebna was that one grew in a manner that was similar to God and the other did not. Eliakim was a mighty one, a hero, a god-like one. While Shebna was not!

Shebna's position of scribe can be viewed as an opportunity to turn from wicked ways. To humble oneself. It is believed according to some Jewish historians that Shebna was forced to leave the court and eventually the nation due to leprosy. What is known for certain is that the Lord brought him down from his lofty position because he grew in a corrupt manner.

For yet a little while, and the wicked shall not be: yea, thou shalt diligently consider his place, and it shall not be.

Psalm 37:10

The wicked often seem to be full of life and vigor. They appear to have strength and force. And we may even be tempted to envy them.

For I was envious at the foolish, when I saw the prosperity of the wicked.

Psalm 73:3

Do not.

"For they shall soon be cut down
like the grass, and wither as the
green herb."

Psalm 37:2

In order to be full of real vigor we must remain
connected to the one who is the source of true life.
Any other connection is a *deception* and it will
cause us to be cut down and wither as the green
herb!

SHEBNA THE SCRIBE
Vigor

And when they had called to the
king, there came out to them
Eliakim the son of Hilkiah, which
was over the household, and
Shebna the scribe, and Joah the son
of Asaph the recorder.

2 Kings 18:18

Week 1

For he shall grow up before him as
a tender plant, and as a root out of
a dry ground: he hath no form nor
comeliness; and when we shall see
him, there is no beauty that we
should desire him.

Isaiah 53:2

When we are young or even new to something we are at our most vulnerable. Extreme care is needed in order to be preserve and to foster healthy growth. Mixed in is excitement and zeal, which at times can override sound judgment. It can cause us to make rash decisions or not to look at a matter clearly or in depth. It is at these times that the Lord alone should lay our foundation.

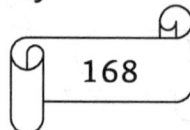

168

Nevertheless, the firm foundation
of God stands, having this seal,
"The Lord knows those who are
His," and, "Everyone who names
the name of the Lord is to abstain
from wickedness."

2 Timothy 2:19

WEEK 1

Are there people that you envy who seem to prosper in their ways? How has it influenced your thoughts, actions, and emotions?

PRAYER

Father, help me not to be envious of evil doers. Let me not look at them with the eye of longing or wishing. Help me to focus on laying the right foundation in you. That there are no cracks in my foundation floor or wall. That my motives are pure and true. Lord, help me to study what you desire I focus on. Let me not be carried away by looking at others. Sanctify my heart and life. Put the right spirit within me in the name of Jesus, amen.

Shebna the Scribe
Vigor

And when they had called to the
king, there came out to them
Eliakim the son of Hilkiah, which
was over the household, and
Shebna the scribe, and Joah the son
of Asaph the recorder.

2 Kings 18:18

Week 2

For he shall grow up before him as
a tender plant, and as a root out of
a dry ground: he hath no form nor
comeliness; and when we shall see
him, there is no beauty that we
should desire him.

Isaiah 53:2

In Isaiah 22, we get an account of what happened to Shebna and why. The Lord had spoken a word that Judah and Jerusalem would be carried away. They did not believe it. They had confidence in their power and ability to keep themselves safe from attack. They prepared their walls and made sure they had water to withstand a siege. They invested heavily in the works and abilities of their own hands rather than to repent before God. Although they prepared the favor of the Lord was not upon them. He was not going to deliver them.

Shebna was so confident that he would not be carried away into exile that he built for himself an *elaborate tomb*. He was full of arrogance and pride that the Lord had to ask him "Who do you think you are? What do you think you have? You really are nothing and you have nothing" (Isaiah 22:15-17).

Because of his pride God made sure that, he died in exile. He was tossed like a ball into a large country destined to live out his days in shame (Isaiah 22:17-19). The judgment of God on Shebna was complete for he was stripped of his position, honor and authority. Another was raised to take his place.

Humbleness is a requirement when working for the Lord. The ability to discern is also crucial. Shebna had neither. He was full of vigor but it was nothing in comparison to the vigor of God. He had energy but he lacked the spirit of the fear of the Lord. His pride blinded him to the true state of things and so it made him fall.

Pride goeth before destruction,
and an haughty spirit before a fall.

Proverbs 16:18

WEEK 2

As you consider your life this week, how would you assess your growth pattern? Are you growing in the ways of the Lord or are you advancing in a crooked or corrupt manner? If corrupt, are you willing to do something to change that? If in the ways of the Lord, are you willing to affirm your commitment to continuing the course? How well acquainted are you with the spirits of humbleness and obedience?

PRAYER

What would you like God to do for you this week? What things do you need to repent for? Write out your prayer and release it unto the Lord believing that he will do as you have asked. If you are not sure what to ask for seek guidance from Holy Spirit that is a sure way to know that you are not praying amiss.

Kingdom Scribes
Seeking the Scribes Anointing
SHEBNA THE SCRIBE
Vigor

And when they had called to the
king, there came out to them
Eliakim the son of Hilkiah, which
was over the household, and
Shebna the scribe, and Joah the son
of Asaph the recorder.

2 Kings 18:18

Week 3

For he shall grow up before him as
a tender plant, and as a root out of
a dry ground: he hath no form nor
comeliness; and when we shall see
him, there is no beauty that we
should desire him.

Isaiah 53:2

As living souls, we possess certain level of *strength* or *force.* We are able to move things or accomplish tasks although each of us may have a different level of vigor we each possess it because God has given it to us.

When we are born, we start out as seeds planted in the fertile and rich soil of the earth. The enemy has everything waiting and ready to entice us and

177

to ensnare us into the corrupt ways of the world. His goal is to ensure that we are deeply rooted in the ways of sin and iniquity so that this will be our only point of reference. It would be our reality for it would be familiar.

When we become born again, we are once more like seeds or babes. Once more, we begin as sapling or suckling's. The difference being that this time we are trying to grow in the dry or drought earth by the grace of God.

Our strength, firmness, and vigor is to come from the spiritual ground of the Lord. What we need to grow will not come from the parched earth.

The Lord himself will ensure that we increase (1 Corinthians 3:6-8).

But whosoever drinketh of the water that I shall give him shall never thirst; but the water that I shall give him shall be in him a well of water springing up into everlasting life.

John 4:14

WEEK 3

Have you desired spiritual fruit but planted in earthly soil? Are you willing to dig up the old to plant something new? Are you rightly aligned with Jesus to get your fill of water?

PRAYER

Father, I do not know what to do. I do not know where to go. I ask that you take me by the hand and lead me. I desire have within me a well of water springing up into eternal life. Help me in Jesus name I pray, amen.

SHEBNA THE SCRIBE
Vigor

And when they had called to the
king, there came out to them
Eliakim the son of Hilkiah, which
was over the household, and
Shebna the scribe, and Joah the son
of Asaph the recorder.

2 Kings 18:18

Week 4

For he shall grow up before him as
a tender plant, and as a root out of
a dry ground: he hath no form nor
comeliness; and when we shall see
him, there is no beauty that we
should desire him.

Isaiah 53:2

Isaiah 53:2 speaks of how Christ would come to the earth. He would come as a young plant one that could be shaped. Although he would have a root that was the root of the spirit, he would be growing out of a parched, drought, or a dry area. He would come without shape. He would not have the honor of a position nor would he be adorned in splendor to grab our attention.

181

Christ laid aside all in order to reclaim all to the glory of God. He submitted his strength, force, life, and vigor to God in order to be rightly led and trained.

> Though he were a Son, yet learned he obedience by the things which he suffered; And being made perfect, he became the author of eternal salvation unto all them that obey him;
>
> Hebrews 5:8-9

If we desire to grow as tender plants to the glory of God we too must lay aside what we consider important in order to obtain what is genuinely significant in the eyes of God. If we do not the fate that befell Shebna could also befall us.

WEEK 4

What are some of the things that are in the way of your fulfilling the call that God has placed on your life? List them out. Then place it on the altar before God in prayer.

PRAYER

This is your sacrifice before the Lord. Place them before him so they can be consumed and then ask him for what you need in order to be deeply rooted, well watered and fruitful before him.

September

BARUCH THE SCRIBE
Blessed

Then took Jeremiah another roll,
and gave it to Baruch the scribe,
the son of Neriah; who wrote
therein from the mouth of
Jeremiah all the words of the book
which Jehoiakim king of Judah had
burned in the fire: and there were
added besides unto them many
like words.

Jeremiah 36:32

Blessed is the man that walketh
not in the counsel of the ungodly,
nor standeth in the way of sinners,
nor sitteth in the seat of the
scornful.

2 But his delight is in the law of the
Lord; and in his law doth he
meditate day and night.

---

3 And he shall be like a tree
planted by the rivers of water, that
bringeth forth his fruit in his
season; his leaf also shall not
wither; and whatsoever he doeth
shall prosper.

Psalm 1:1-3

he name **Baruch** means *blessed*. Its root
(*barak*) is to kneel, to bless or to cause to
kneel. The Gesenius' Hebrew-Chaldee
Lexicon states that it means to bend the knees, to
ask for a blessing, to invoke God, or to be caused
to prosper by God. The first use of *barak* was in
Genesis 1:22 when God blessed Adam and Eve and
commanded them to be fruitful and multiply.

And God blessed them, and God
said unto them, Be fruitful, and
multiply, and replenish the earth,
and subdue it: and have dominion
over the fish of the sea, and over
the fowl of the air, and over every
living thing that moveth upon the
earth.

Genesis 1:28

187

From the name **Baruch**, we gather important information about what it takes to be blessed by God. God blesses the humble those who are willing to kneel or bow their knees before him.

O come, let us worship and bow down: let us kneel before the LORD our maker.

Psalm 95:6

If we humble ourselves before him, he will prosper us.

Humble yourselves in the sight of the Lord, and he shall lift you up.

James 4:10

If we refuse to humble ourselves before him, he will resist us.

But he giveth more grace. Wherefore he saith, God resisteth the proud, but giveth grace unto the humble.

James 4:6

Baruch was a man who walked in humbleness as he carried out the duties as a scribe to Jeremiah the prophet.

Humbleness evokes more favor from the Lord. Humbleness causes one to thrive, to rejoice exceedingly, to be glad, to experience benefits and bounty and to get rewards from the Lord. Humbleness unlocks the loving-kindness of God. Woven in there is the pleasure, sweetness, delight, lovingness and tender communications with God.

Baruch the Scribe
Blessed

Then took Jeremiah another roll, and gave it to Baruch the scribe, the son of Neriah; who wrote therein from the mouth of Jeremiah all the words of the book which Jehoiakim king of Judah had burned in the fire: and there were added besides unto them many like words.

Jeremiah 36:32

Week 1

Blessed is the man that walketh not in the counsel of the ungodly, nor standeth in the way of sinners, nor sitteth in the seat of the scornful.

2 But his delight is in the law of the Lord; and in his law doth he meditate day and night.

---

3 And he shall be like a tree
planted by the rivers of water, that
bringeth forth his fruit in his
season; his leaf also shall not
wither; and whatsoever he doeth
shall prosper.

Psalm 1:1-3

How can one live a blessed life? How can one be counted among the blessed of the Lord? It can be accomplished by not allowing the ungodly to teach you. The counsel of the ungodly is designed to lead the people astray. Its intent is to cause a perversion in the walk or life of the individual.

Walking signifies a daily activity. It is something that is natural and done often. As we function daily we are to sow seeds of righteousness we are to establish righteousness as we live life. We are to be beacons of light to draw others to the light of Christ that is why our counsel must come from a pure source.

Christ is our pure source he has the seven fold spirits of God, one of which is the spirit of counsel. Christ is always willing to loan us of himself, we can take a loan from him and put to good use the *spirit of counsel*.

191

How often do you have tender communications with God? How often do you enjoy the sweetness of his presence? When was the last time that you delighted in the Lord and felt his delight over you? How willing are you to take a loan of counsel from the Lord? Which areas in your life could benefit from the spirit of counsel?

PRAYER

Lord I am in need of a loan of counsel. Pour it out liberally on me and teach me to walk in the ways of the wise, prepared with a ready and beneficial word in and out of season I pray, amen.

BARUCH THE SCRIBE
Blessed

Then took Jeremiah another roll,
and gave it to Baruch the scribe, the
son of Neriah; who wrote therein
from the mouth of Jeremiah all the
words of the book which Jehoiakim
king of Judah had burned in the fire:
and there were added besides unto
them many like words.

Jeremiah 36:32

Week 2

Blessed is the man that walketh
not in the counsel of the ungodly,
nor standeth in the way of sinners,
nor sitteth in the seat of the
scornful.

2 But his delight is in the law of the
Lord; and in his law doth he
meditate day and night.

---

3 And he shall be like a tree
planted by the rivers of water, that
bringeth forth his fruit in his
season; his leaf also shall not
wither; and whatsoever he doeth
shall prosper.

Psalm 1:1-3

How can we remain blessed of the Lord? To put it simply, **take thy feet and run!** Refuse to stand in the way of sinners. Don't tarry among them. Don't abide or endure long with them. Refuse to stand firmly with them. Maintain a separation between them and yourself. Hold your ground in righteousness. Keep doing what is right in attitude and action. For if, you refuse to run and choose to stand still you will become the servant of sin.

A sinner is one exposed to condemnation. It is a person who has missed the mark and has wandered away from God. It is a person who needs purification from uncleanness. He is guilty and is under the penalty of sin. It is one who forfeit the blessings and benefits of God. One who is without reconciliation. It is one who is in the kingdom of darkness. However, Christ has made a way through repentance and forgiveness for all who desire to be his in spirit and in truth.

14 Be ye not unequally yoked together with unbelievers: for what fellowship hath righteousness with unrighteousness? and what communion hath light with darkness?

15 And what concord hath Christ with Belial? or what part hath he that believeth with an infidel?

16 And what agreement hath the temple of God with idols? for ye are the temple of the living God; as God hath said, I will dwell in them, and walk in them; and I will be their God, and they shall be my people.

17 Wherefore come out from among them, and be ye separate, saith the Lord, and touch not the unclean thing; and I will receive you.

2 Corinthians 6:14-17

In order to remain blessed vigilance is required.

WEEK 2

How vigilant are you over the things that God has entrusted to you? When you notice people doing wrong things what do you do? When you hear them speaking of evil things what do you do? Would God approve of your position or would he counsel you to do something different?

PRAYER

Lord, help me to avoid standing firmly with those rooted and committed to sin. Help me to congregate with those that seek after righteousness. Enable me to be watchful at all times guarding my gates. Anoint my eyes and ears Lord so that they filter and weed out the things that I am exposed to. Cause me to be a blessing in the earth I pray, amen.

BARUCH THE SCRIBE
Blessed

---

*Then took Jeremiah another roll,
and gave it to Baruch the scribe, the
son of Neriah; who wrote therein
from the mouth of Jeremiah all the
words of the book which Jehoiakim
king of Judah had burned in the fire:
and there were added besides unto
them many like words.*

Jeremiah 36:32

Week 3

Blessed is the man that walketh
not in the counsel of the ungodly,
nor standeth in the way of sinners,
nor sitteth in the seat of the
scornful.

2 But his delight is in the law of the
Lord; and in his law doth he
meditate day and night.

---

3 And he shall be like a tree
planted by the rivers of water, that
bringeth forth his fruit in his
season; his leaf also shall not
wither; and whatsoever he doeth
shall prosper.

Psalm 1:1-3

In Psalm 1 we see the progressive pattern of corruption. It starts with speech, with simple advice or a consultation. It could be to devise a plan or to deliberate. No matter what the cause for the discussion it offers the possibility of an open door. It could be the opportunity sin is looking for in order to derail your walk.

Next, there is walking with the sinful. The Bible asks a very simple but profound question in the book of Amos.

Can two walk together, except
they be agreed?

Amos 3:3

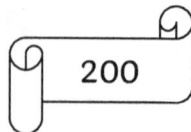

This the million dollar question. The person may be a bundle of laughs. They may be sweeter than sweet potato pie, but their nature is compromised. They serve another and the other is the enemy of your soul (Peter 5:8).

The last step is to get you to sit with them. To have lunch or dinner with them which is not hurried. It is to dwell, abide, or to remain. The story of the young and old prophet in 1 Kings is a wonderful reminder of the hidden dangers of sins progressive pattern of corruption (1 Kings 13:11-25). If we are not careful, it could cost us everything and/or terminate our lives prematurely. The young prophet paid the ultimate price.

As you reflect on your life (relationships) do you, see evidence of sins corruptive pattern? At what stage is it? How will you proceed from this point?

PRAYER

What specifically do you want God to do for you? What areas do you need assistance? What virtues would you like to grow? Lift it up before the Lord.

BARUCH THE SCRIBE
Blessed

---

*Then took Jeremiah another roll,
and gave it to Baruch the scribe, the
son of Neriah; who wrote therein
from the mouth of Jeremiah all the
words of the book which Jehoiakim
king of Judah had burned in the fire:
and there were added besides unto
them many like words.*

Jeremiah 36:32

Week 4

Blessed is the man that walketh
not in the counsel of the ungodly,
nor standeth in the way of sinners,
nor sitteth in the seat of the
scornful.

2 But his delight is in the law of the
Lord; and in his law doth he
meditate day and night.

---

3 And he shall be like a tree
planted by the rivers of water, that
bringeth forth his fruit in his
season; his leaf also shall not
wither; and whatsoever he doeth
shall prosper.

Psalm 1:1-3

People delight in many things, but what does it mean to delight in the law of the Lord? To delight in something is to be pleased to do, to take pleasure in, to move or bend toward, to will or find favorable. Those that desire to be blessed and to be a blessing will, **will themselves** to find pleasure in the law of God. At the root of delight is choice. They choose to find pleasure and delight in the instruction of God.

The instructions of God are teachings, directions, counsel, and a template for life. However at the root of the law of God is an arsenal of arrows that pierce the eye or understanding. It possesses aggressive wrestling tactics to throw down the enemy. It is teaching by example and counsel. It is directing others by pointing out or showing something. It is to throw water or to rain as in the former and latter rain (Joel 2:23).

The law of God is equipped with everything we needed to teach, battle, plant, counsel, and reason. By studying the word of God, it allows us to flow as *living* water.

He that believeth on me, as the scripture hath said, out of his belly shall flow rivers of living water.

John 7:38

WEEK 4

How often do you meditate on the word of God? How well are you furnishing others with living water?

Father cause my belly to flow with rivers of living water in the name of Jesus. (**Add your own prayer points so that god can meet your need abundantly**).

October

Zadok the scribe
Righteous

And I made treasurers over the treasuries, Shelemiah the priest, and Zadok the scribe, and of the Levites, Pedaiah: and next to them was Hanan the son of Zaccur, the son of Mattaniah: for they were counted faithful, and their office was to distribute unto their brethren.

Nehemiah 13:13

He that walketh uprightly, and worketh righteousness, and speaketh the truth in his heart.

Psalm 15:2

Zadok was a scribe appointed by Nehemiah as one of the treasurers over the storehouse of God. His name means *righteous*. At its root, it is to be straight, right, and just. It is to be declared righteous, vindicated or saved from wrongs. It is to be made righteous. Woven within the name **Zadok** is the notion of speaking the truth and saying what is right. Carrying oneself uprightly. However, it also conveys the notion of

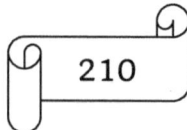

the responsibility of work, the work of purging oneself from suspicion as in Genesis 44:16.

The name **Zadok** is a *weighty* name for in it is the weight and meaning of what it is to be righteous. It communicates what God looks for and considers righteousness.

> He who walks in his uprightness
> fears the LORD, But he who is
> devious in his ways despises Him.
>
> Proverbs 14:2

When we walk in uprightness, it shows that we respect and reverence the Lord. But when we do not it communicates that we despise God.

As scribes, we have a choice as to how we will continue to grow with God. He does not take the power of choice away from us however, if we desire to grow in the scribes anointing we should choose to do what pleases him and eliminate was does not.

> Do good, O LORD, to those who are
> good And to those who are upright
> in their hearts.
>
> Psalm 125:4

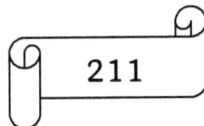

Zadok the scribe
Righteous

---

*And I made treasurers over the
treasuries, Shelemiah the priest, and
Zadok the scribe, and of the Levites,
Pedaiah: and next to them was
Hanan the son of Zaccur, the son of
Mattaniah: for they were counted
faithful, and their office was to
distribute unto their brethren.*

Nehemiah 13:13

Week 1

He that walketh uprightly, and
worketh righteousness, and
speaketh the truth in his heart.

Psalm 15:2

Zadok was the son of **Ahitub**. The name **Ahitub** means *my brother is goodness*. At the root of Ahitub's name is to be pleasing and joyful, to do good, act right and to be of benefit.

As scribes, we are to be of benefit to the kingdom of God. Our focus is to sow goodness wherever we go. God is a good God. Although this has become a catch phrase of late, it does not negate the fact that our God is truly good. When people encounter you are they pleased and thankful for the encounter? Do they look forward to your next meeting?

If you were to be taken home today, what would they say about the life that you have led? Would they say you were upright in all your ways, that you sowed goodness at each opportunity? Would they recount the many ways you were beneficial to them.

God chose you to advance his agenda. He expects you to live up to the righteous call that he placed on your life. He expects that you will be of benefit to the kingdom. You are a tool in his hands and he is using you to create a new reality in a darkened world. As an engraver uses engraving tools, the Lord is using you to engrave the world around you.

How do you feel about that? How do you sow goodness?

With fairness, discernment, beauty, love,
generosity, kindness, understanding, and
wisdom, by looking out for the welfare of others,
caring, forgiving, hoping, praying, nurturing,
teaching, encouraging, and having patience.

For the LORD is righteous, He loves
righteousness; The upright will
behold His face.

Psalm 11:7

WEEK 1

In what ways have you sown goodness? Righteousness? How can you sow more seeds of righteousness? Goodness? How can you implement increased sowing this week?

PRAYER

What do you want God to do for you this week? What things specifically do you want him to increase so that you can grow in righteousness and in goodness? Ask him for open doors of opportunity to sow abundantly to the glory of God.

Write your prayer below.

ZADOK THE SCRIBE
Righteous

And I made treasurers over the
treasuries, Shelemiah the priest,
and Zadok the scribe, and of the
Levites, Pedaiah: and next to them
was Hanan the son of Zaccur, the
son of Mattaniah: for they were
counted faithful, and their office
was to distribute unto their
brethren.

Nehemiah 13:13

Week 2

He that walketh uprightly, and
worketh righteousness, and
speaketh the truth in his heart.

Psalm 15:2

Zadok the scribe was a man of righteousness. He came from a father acquainted with goodness. In Psalm 15, David outlines what it will take for a person to dwell in the temple of the Lord. In Revelation 3:12, Christ states that those who overcome (meaning to bring in the victory for God) will be a pillar in the temple of God and they will never leave it.

So what will it take to reside as a pillar in the temple of God forever?

David outlines it as walking uprightly, working righteousness, not backbiting with our tongue, doing no evil to our neighbor, not criticizing our fellow citizens in order to exalt ourselves. Not looking at others with distain (despising them) or counting them as worthless.

He that speaking truth in our inward part (heart), and does not take bribes to lie against the innocent, or lend money at an outrageous interest rate (usury). He that is willing to take an oath to his own hurt and not recant.

It is easy to pretend that we are righteous for many Pharisees and Sadducees did it for centuries; however, they were unable to fool Jesus or John the Baptist (Matthew 23:33, Luke 3:1-9). Likewise, we will not be able to fool Christ or those who are discerning.

As scribes, our utmost desires should *be to be as God is* without pretense or falsehood. The checklist of David is a wonderful place to start for self-examination. We can lie and deceive others but in our hearts, we know the truth and if we don't then we need to ask Holy Spirit to reveal the true condition of our hearts, to lay it bare. Self-deception is worse than ignorance for it involves lying to yourself and believing the lie while ignorance is lack of knowledge (Hosea 4:6).

Kingdom Scribes
Seeking the Scribes Anointing

As scribes, we have access to the Spirit of Knowledge through Christ Jesus, the possessor of the sevenfold spirit of God (Revelation 3:1). The only way to deal with a lie is to **overthrow** it with truth.

Are you ready to examine your inward parts?

Unto the upright there ariseth
light in the darkness: he is
gracious, and full of compassion,
and righteous.

Psalm 112:4

How well are you walking before God? Are you on the right course to spend eternity in the presence of Jehovah? How can you establish truth in your heart? What lies need to be uprooted?

PRAYER

Holy Spirit you are the spirit of truth help me to know the condition of my heart. Help me to establish truth in my inward parts. Lead me where I need to go. Direct my eyes so that I can see what has been hidden in the darkness. Shine the light of Jesus and illuminate every recessed corner of my being. It is my earnest desire to walk righteously before you. Help me I pray, in Jesus name, amen.

But of him are ye in Christ Jesus, who of God is made unto us wisdom, and righteousness, and sanctification, and redemption:

1 Corinthians 1:30

ZADOK THE SCRIBE
Righteous

And I made treasurers over the treasuries, Shelemiah the priest, and Zadok the scribe, and of the Levites, Pedaiah: and next to them was Hanan the son of Zaccur, the son of Mattaniah: for they were counted faithful, and their office was to distribute unto their brethren.

Nehemiah 13:13

Week 3

He that walketh uprightly, and worketh righteousness, and speaketh the truth in his heart.

Psalm 15:2

As scribes of the kingdom, we should be willing to converse with ourselves. But what does that mean? It is to speak truthfully to ourselves by warning, promising, commanding, threatening, singing, or declaring. It is to help lead us away from evil and put to flight wrong doings. It is the function of bringing ourselves into the right order so that we can lead others and ourselves in righteousness and truth.

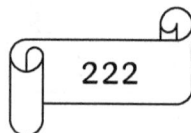

222

When we talk to ourselves in truth it subdues the enemy and pulls his ensnarement's down. It also exposes the enemy's schemes in the light.

Our inner parts are comprised of our mind, soul, heart, understanding, will, conscience, passions, emotions, intelligence, courage, character, resolutions, reflections, memory, determination as well as our appetites. It is the totality of our conscious being. How well are you fashioning it for the Lord? How well are you guarding it from the enemy?

Good and upright is the LORD:
therefore will he teach sinners in
the way.

The meek will he guide in
judgment: and the meek will he
teach his way.

All the paths of the LORD are
mercy and truth unto such as keep
his covenant and his testimonies.

Psalm 25:8-10

WEEK 3

How often do you listen to the conversations that you have with yourself? Is what you say to yourself true, virtuous, and upright? Do you view yourself and others through the lens of God? Are your conversations full of life or death (Proverbs 18:21)?

PRAYER

Father, forgive me for speaking words that are not full of life and faith. Fill my mouth with words of virtue, life, power and love. Help me to speak life words to myself. Grow me in life to fulfill the purpose of Christ. Lord, I call out for life, I cry out for abundant life. Lord, do your work in my inward parts in the name of Jesus. Make me fruitful and abundant in all things. I am called of you prosper me in every undertaking to your honor and glory I pray, amen.

For he hath made him to be sin for
us, who knew no sin; that we
might be made the righteousness
of God in him.

2 Corinthians 5:21

ZADOK THE SCRIBE
Righteous

---

*And I made treasurers over the
treasuries, Shelemiah the priest, and
Zadok the scribe, and of the Levites,
Pedaiah: and next to them was
Hanan the son of Zaccur, the son of
Mattaniah: for they were counted
faithful, and their office was to
distribute unto their brethren.*

Nehemiah 13:13

Week 4

---

*He that walketh uprightly, and
worketh righteousness, and speaketh
the truth in his heart.*

Psalm 15:2

What does it mean to be counted faithful? The Hebrew meaning for the phrase is to be considered, to be thought of, esteemed or regarded as faithful.

The men in Nehemiah 13:13 were considered to be firm, unshaken, sure, and trustworthy. Nehemiah was able to depend on them. They were as firm pillars of support. He was able to confide in them and lean upon them. The

Gesenius' Hebrew-Chaldee Lexicon tells us that they had long continuance as a perennial. They were healthy and were workers able to build up the work of God.

What a testament! To be found faithful to do the work entrusted to you. In order for these men to get such an honorable mention, they had to be confirmed and verified as faithful. This is a starch contrast to what happens in our present day. Often people get accolades and honors without being vetted. Connections speak louder than character. It speaks louder than consistency. And it often speaks louder than truth.

As scribes of the kingdom, we are to pursue truth. If accolades are given, at its **root should be truth**. It is easy to appear as a shining star in isolated instances but how do you hold up over time? Are you reliable, trustworthy, and faithful? Do you help to build or tear down? Are you a faithful support to others? Can God rely on you to help him build and advance the kingdom in the hearts and minds of men?

Nehemiah assembled a group of men who had similar natures as such they were able to stand firm, create an atmosphere of righteousness, and advance the vision and purpose of God. If we look at their names we find *repaid by Jehovah* (**Shelemiah**), *righteous* (**Zadok**), *Jehovah ransomed* (**Pedaiah**), *he is merciful* (**Hanan**), *mindful* (**Zaccur**), and *gift of Jehovah* (**Mattaniah** from

Zaccur's father). God declared what he was doing and why throughout the administration of Nehemiah. These men were brought together by the divine design of God as beautiful constellation to declare the handy work of God in the midst their enemies. As Jehovah did it for them, he will do for us if we are willing to live up to the call he has placed on our lives.

The righteous shall be glad in the LORD, and shall trust in him; and all the upright in heart shall glory.

Psalm 64:10

WEEK 4

Are you reliable, trustworthy, and faithful? Do you help to build or tear down? Are you a faithful support to others? Can God rely on you to help him build and advance the kingdom in the hearts and minds of men?

PRAYER

Father ,in the name of Jesus, I come believing that you have a divine plan for my life. Connect me with those who I am assigned to support and encourage. Link me with those who are to support and encourage me. Lord hold us together in a bond of love. Love for you and for each other. Lord fill us with the desire to see your handy work displayed in our lives and in the work you have given us to do. I ask these mercies in the name of Jesus, amen.

November

SHAVSHA THE SCRIBE
Nobility

And Zadok the son of Ahitub, and
Abimelech the son of Abiathar,
were the priests; and Shavsha was
scribe;

1 Chronicles 18:16

Yea, I will rejoice over them to do
them good, and I will plant them
in this land assuredly with my
whole heart and with my whole
soul.

Jeremiah 32:41

Shavsha was the scribe for King David. His name means nobility. It's root meaning is to exult, rejoice, to be glad and to display joy. Just by his name alone, he sounds like a happy person and he was in the administration of one who enjoyed worshipping and praising Jehovah. He was the royal secretary of the one who was credited by God as having a heart after his own heart (Acts 13:22).

The real point of interest in **Shavsha's** name is that when we examine scriptures that use the same root word *suws* (rejoice) we see that it is God rejoicing over his people as well as his people rejoicing over him.

Yea, I will rejoice over them to do them good, and I will plant them in this land assuredly with my whole heart and with my whole soul.

Jeremiah 32:41

When God rejoices over his people, he is provoked to do good unto them. It releases an overflow of goodness. God holds nothing back. However, in order for his goodness to flow divine order and cleansing must take place.

Jeremiah 32 gives us a glimpse into what God does so that he can rejoice over his people and release the floodgates of goodness upon them.

God will gather his people together in safety. He will once more call them his people and he will be their God. He will give them one heart, one way, so they will fear, respect and honor him continually into the following generations. He will provide an everlasting agreement with them so that he will be their God. Once all of this is put in place God will rejoice over his people.

God identified the problem and provided the best solution so that he could rejoice and do good to his people. As a scribe of God, have you been scattered by the Lord for doing what displeases him? If you have examine his solution to your problem. Possessing a god-like heart, Gods ways, a spirit that has the fear of the Lord, the spirit of the Lord, acknowledging that God is Lord.

When was the last time God had cause to rejoice over you? What will you do to ensure that he continually rejoices over you?

And I will rejoice in Jerusalem, and joy in my people: and the voice of weeping shall be no more heard in her, nor the voice of crying.

Isaiah 65:19

SHAVSHA THE SCRIBE
Nobility

And Zadok the son of Ahitub, and
Abimelech the son of Abiathar,
were the priests; and Shavsha was
scribe;

1 Chronicles 18:16

Week 1

Yea, I will rejoice over them to do
them good, and I will plant them
in this land assuredly with my
whole heart and with my whole
soul.

Jeremiah 32:41

Rejoice *forever* in what God creates! Behold his creations. God is always doing something new. He is continually shaping and fashioning things just the way he wants them. In Isaiah 65, he counsels us to behold his creation. He created "Jerusalem a rejoicing." As a circle of peace.

Jerusalem means teaching of peace. However, its core meaning is to throw or shoot arrows, to instruct, direct, show, point out and to throw

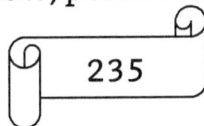

water (rain). Within its meaning, it has to lay, cast and set something.

And when ye see this, your heart
shall rejoice, and your bones shall
flourish like an herb: and the hand
of the LORD shall be known
toward his servants, and his
indignation toward his enemies.

Isaiah 66:14

In the name **Jerusalem,** we have the work of God identified so that we can grasp part of the scope of his vision for his people. These are tactics, they are strategies. Not every situation will require the same approach but according to the need the *teaching of peace* can meet the occasion. If it is through war and battle arrows will be shot. If it is thought schooling, teaching will commence. If it is through watering because seeds have been planted rain or water will be poured. If direction is needed a way will be pointed out. If the wrong path has been taken the *teaching of peace* will encourage the individual to lay it aside.

> But be ye glad and rejoice for ever
> in that which I create: for, behold, I
> create Jerusalem a rejoicing, and
> her people a joy.
>
> Isaiah 65:18

But Jerusalem has an even deeper meaning. It is a covenant of peace between God and his people. It is to live in peace, to be sound, to be kept safe, to know that God will finish what he has started and will perform all he said he would do. It is the assurance that God is on your side and will repay, restore and compensate his people justly.

God fashions universes, nations, people and situations. He transforms them into what is better. He causes his creation to rejoice (Luke 19:40).

> I will praise thee; for I am fearfully
> and wonderfully made:
> marvellous are thy works; and that
> my soul knoweth right well.
>
> Psalm 139:14

Let the heavens rejoice, and let the
earth be glad; let the sea roar, and
the fulness thereof. 12 Let the field
be joyful, and all that is therein:
then shall all the trees of the wood
rejoice

Psalm 96:11-12

The Hebrew root meaning for *rejoicing* is a circle. It also has the notion of trembling, exulting and to be glad. The enemies of God will tremble when he rejoices over his people. They will tremble when the people of God rejoice over their creator. To surround yourself with delight in the Lord is to have it encamped round about you. It is to crown yourself with a crown of joy. It is to establish that God is over all. And that in the midst of your rejoicing all other things must bow. Rejoicing is a resisting strategy, it is active so that we are not overtaken by the enemy (1 Samuel 16:23, James 4:7).

WEEK 1

Has your head been cast down because of rejections? Lack of inspiration? Writers block? Life? How about starting with praise, worship, or rejoicing?

PRAYER

Whatever your issue is list them and turn them into praise, rejoicing, worship before the Lord. Pray them. Sing them. Declare them. Use them as weapons of warfare against the enemy who is trying to create a different reality for you. Praise Jehovah for he is creating something in you dear scribe. Something new. You are a rejoicing. You are a joy!

SHAVSHA THE SCRIBE
Nobility

And Zadok the son of Ahitub, and
Abimelech the son of Abiathar,
were the priests; and Shavsha was
scribe;

1 Chronicles 18:16

Week 2

Yea, I will rejoice over them to do
them good, and I will plant them
in this land assuredly with my
whole heart and with my whole
soul.

Jeremiah 32:41

As a scribe, you are nobility. You are in a sense the royal scribe of the Lord. He has fashioned you and created your position. He has given you a purpose and instructions on how to accomplish your mission. Therefore, as with **Shavsha** you are to rejoice and exult the Lord. You are to display joy for the Lord has created YOU!

According to Jeremiah 32, God has planted you in the land. He has placed you where you are so that he can rejoice over you. He has fixed you so that you will rejoice in him.

To be planted is to be rooted, grounded, fixed, established, and fastened in. Jehovah has done this for you. In your midst is the Lord. He has made his home with you. And he has made a way for you to be with him in his.

And hath raised us up together, and made us sit together in heavenly places in Christ Jesus:

Ephesians 2:6

Rejoice for he is good to you. Rejoice for he continues to fashion new things for you. Rejoice for he will complete what he has started. Rejoice!

WEEK 2

How are you feeling right now? What things are you rejoicing over? What things would you like to rejoice over? What is the condition of your heart right now?

PRAYER

Is your heart flowing with joy, gratitude, appreciation, awe, reverence, love, affection, happiness, humbleness, peace, thankfulness etc? Tell the Lord about it. Why are you grateful that he chose you as his scribe? Why are you grateful for where he has planted you?

Let all those that seek thee rejoice and be glad in thee: and let such as love thy salvation say continually, Let God be magnified.

Psalm 70:4

Let all those that seek thee rejoice and be glad in thee: let such as love thy salvation say continually, The Lord be magnified.

Psalm 40:16

SHAVSHA THE SCRIBE
Nobility

And Zadok the son of Ahitub, and
Abimelech the son of Abiathar,
were the priests; and Shavsha was
scribe;

1 Chronicles 18:16

Week 3

Yea, I will rejoice over them to do
them good, and I will plant them
in this land assuredly with my
whole heart and with my whole
soul.

Jeremiah 32:41

If God were to bless all our income, yield, crops, products of your lips, revenue and gains how would you feel? What would you do? If he were to take it a step further and bless all the works of your hands what would you think? What would be your next act?

Seven days shalt thou keep a
solemn feast unto the LORD thy
God in the place, which the LORD
shall choose: because the LORD thy
God shall bless thee in all thine
increase, and in all the works of
thine hands, therefore thou shalt
surely rejoice.

Deuteronomy 16:15

This is what he promised to do for his children. Then he declared, "Thou shalt surely rejoice." What does it mean to surely rejoice?

You will *definitely be merry*. You will *absolutely be glad*. You will *undoubtedly exult*. You will *be gladdened*. You will be *caused to rejoice*.

When the Lord does good unto his people the response he desires is rejoicing. He wants us to have a cheerful countenance. Bright faces and merry voices.

When the Lord corrects us or denies us we should respond in the same manner; for it is out of his goodness and love that he corrects or withholds.

Kingdom Scribes
Seeking the Scribes Anointing

As his noble scribes, we know that God always does what is best for those he loves. And because we are loved with an everlasting love, we continually have cause to rejoice in the goodness of our God!

WEEK 3

Read over the scripture below and identify the things in your life that you are exceedingly thankful for. Then pray or sing them to the Lord.

But let the righteous be glad; let them rejoice before God: yea, let them exceedingly rejoice.

Psalm 68:3

PRAYER

Record your song as a memo or write it out here so that you can have a memorial of what you released unto the Lord today. You exceedingly rejoiced before Jehovah.

M. J. Welcome

SHAVSHA THE SCRIBE
Nobility

And Zadok the son of Ahitub, and
Abimelech the son of Abiathar,
were the priests; and Shavsha was
scribe;

1 Chronicles 18:16

Week 4

Yea, I will rejoice over them to do
them good, and I will plant them
in this land assuredly with my
whole heart and with my whole
soul.

Jeremiah 32:41

It is easy to rejoice in the Lord when he has given us the things that we longed for or prayed for. It is easy to be glad when all is going well or we experienced a breakthrough moment. How often do we thank him for his word? Thank him for his testimonies? Thank him for just being God?

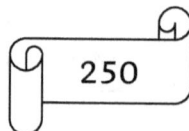

I rejoice at thy word, as one that
findeth great spoil.

Psalm 119:162

David did. He absolutely got the fact that as a noble we are to rejoice and exult the Lord. We are to treasure his word above spoils or rewards. The word of God is life, it is food, and it is nourishment.

But he answered and said, It is written, Man shall not live by bread alone, but by every word that proceeds out of the mouth of God.

Matthew 4:4

For the word of God is quick, and powerful, and sharper than any twoedged sword, piercing even to the dividing asunder of soul and spirit, and of the joints and marrow, and is a discerner of the thoughts and intents of the heart.

Hebrews 4:12

Moreover he said unto me, Son of man, eat that thou findest; eat this roll, and go speak unto the house of Israel. 2So I opened my mouth, and he caused me to eat that roll. 3And he said unto me, Son of man, cause thy belly to eat, and fill thy bowels with this roll that I give thee. Then did I eat it; and it was in my mouth as honey for sweetness.

Ezekiel 3:1-3

Kingdom Scribes
Seeking the Scribes Anointing

As noble scribes of the Lord, we are to commit ourselves to digesting the word of God, treasuring it above other things, living in sheer awe of our amazing Father and Lord. It is through our life application that we will be empowered to teach and lead others to the Lord with steadfast and uncorrupted determination. He will rejoice over us as we continue to rejoice over him.

WEEK 4

Take a look at Psalm 119:14. Is this true for you? What do you need to do to make it true or consistently true for you? Lift up your petition before God. Ask so that you can receive.

I have rejoiced in the way of thy testimonies, as much as in all riches.

Psalm 119:14

PRAYER

Based on what you identified above lift up your petition to the Lord. Be bold and confident. God wants to bless you. He wants to plant you. He desires the best for you. You are his chosen scribe and he wants you to do exceedingly well.

December

Shaphan the Scribe
Rock Badger

And the king commanded Hilkiah
the priest, and Ahikam the son of
Shaphan, and Achbor the son of
Michaiah, and Shaphan the scribe,
and Asahiah a servant of the
king's, saying,

2 Kings 22:12

They shall call the people unto the
mountain; there they shall offer
sacrifices of righteousness: for
they shall suck of the abundance
of the seas, and of treasures hid in
the sand.

Deuteronomy 33:19

Shaphan was the scribe of king Josiah of
Judah. He was the father of Ahikam, Elasah,
Gemaiah, and Jaasaniah. He was a faithful
man. His name means rock badger, hyrax, or
coney. These animals are remarkably shrewd.
They are small and are hoofed mammals. They
are said to function in *egalitarian* groups,
following the rule that "the friend of my friend is

my friend rule." They avoid imbalances in their social relationships (Wikipedia, the free encyclopedia). It is interesting to note that higher ranked rock badgers tend to sing more often than others do. It has been stated that they are not a mighty species but they make their homes in the cliffs. Although small, they are wise.

> The conies [are but] a feeble folk, yet make they their houses in the rocks;
>
> Proverbs 30:26

When we look at the root meaning of **Shaphan** we learn that he had the ability to cover over, panel, hide, or treasure up things. He stored precious gems in his heart.

> And Hilkiah the high priest said unto Shaphan the scribe, I have found the book of the law in the house of the LORD. And Hilkiah gave the book to Shaphan, and he read it.
>
> 2 Kings 22:8

When **Shaphan** was made aware of what the newly discovered law-book said by the high priest Hilkiah he read it for himself. Then he read it before the king. Although he was sent on a different errand initially by the king when he was made aware of Gods judgement on Judah he did not remain silent.

And Shaphan the scribe shewed the king, saying, Hilkiah the priest hath delivered me a book. And Shaphan read it before the king.

And it came to pass, when the king had heard the words of the book of the law, that he rent his clothes.

2 Kings 22:10-11

The news he delivered to the king was severe and distressing for the king tore his clothes into pieces. Here we see that **Shaphan** was a loyal scribe to the king for he did not keep the hard news from him but shared the truth with him. He demonstrated strength in character and love, for to love is to speak and share truth. (Psalm 25:5, John 16:13, John 14:6).

SHAPHAN THE SCRIBE
Rock Badger

And the king commanded Hilkiah
the priest, and Ahikam the son of
Shaphan, and Achbor the son of
Michaiah, and Shaphan the scribe,
and Asahiah a servant of the
king's, saying,

2 Kings 22:12

Week 1

They shall call the people unto the
mountain; there they shall offer
sacrifices of righteousness: for
they shall suck of the abundance
of the seas, and of treasures hid in
the sand.

Deuteronomy 33:19

In 2 Kings 22:10, the Bible says, that **Shaphan** shewed the king the book that Hilkiah the priest had given to him. The word **shewed** means to declare, proclaim, publish, report or announce. It also means to acknowledge, inform and to confess in the sight of. It is to *bring to the light*. From this, we understand that the judgment of God was hidden in darkness. Although the book was there, it was concealed. It was brought to light only when King Josiah wanted to repair the temple of God.

As scribes, the Lord uses us to bring things to light in a dark world. We are to shine the light of his message in all that we do. It may be the message that someone needs in order to be motivated to repent or encouraged to do more for the Lord. Even when the message is a hard truth, we are not to second-guess God we are to do what he has commissioned us to do.

WEEK 1

Have there been times when you avoided telling someone the truth because you felt it was harsh or distressing? In light of what Shaphan did, would you have done the same? If you could do things over how would you handle it?

PRAYER

When confronted with truth we have a choice as scribes to either embrace it, ignore it or deny it. If you have handled a situation in the past poorly, what will you do now to make it right in the eyes of God? Let God know your plan through prayer. If moved to make amends with someone you did not love in truth ask Holy Spirit to fill your mouth with the right words and to set the atmosphere so that God is glorified in the name of Jesus.

SHAPHAN THE SCRIBE
Rock Badger

And the king commanded Hilkiah
the priest, and Ahikam the son of
Shaphan, and Achbor the son of
Michaiah, and Shaphan the scribe,
and Asahiah a servant of the
king's, saying,

2 Kings 22:12

Week 2

They shall call the people unto the
mountain; there they shall offer
sacrifices of righteousness: for
they shall suck of the abundance
of the seas, and of treasures hid in
the sand.

Deuteronomy 33:19

B ased on the report of **Shaphan**, King Josiah rose up and started to cleanse the land from idolatry. He was zealous for the Lord. Tearing down shrines, putting down idolatrous priests, burning groves, breaking down houses that were by the house of the Lord, taking back horses that were given to the sun (god) and burning down chariots of the sun, beating down altars, breaking in pieces images, removing bones from sepulchers and burning them upon the altar, and he slew all priests of the high places.

He had the people renew their covenant with God and held a Passover feast. However, all that he did, did not change God's mind. God in his mercy told King Josiah that he would not be alive to see what was to happen; he would be gathered unto his fathers.

What is interesting is that King Josiah rose up. Shaphan's first sons name **Ahikam** means *my brother has risen up*. It means to impose, set, or to make binding. His name speaks of what King Josiah did. He imposed new protocols; he bound the people to God in recommitment to the covenant.

The Gesenius' Hebrew-Chaldee Lexicon gives further insight into the meaning of **Ahikam**. It is to arise, build up, preserve alive, to erect or rise up one fallen down, to set up again, and to establish anything. This is what King Josiah did based on what Shaphan shared with him.

The Law of God was knocked down and he raised it up. He followed David his father doing what was right in the sight of God.

And he did that which was right in
the sight of the LORD, and walked
in all the way of David his father,
and turned not aside to the right
hand or to the left.

2 Kings 22:2

Sometimes we can do what is right but the
situation may not change. We can share what is
pleasing to God but the hearts of the people may
be hardened. Because people may go through the
motion of conversion does not mean they are
converted from the heart. As a scribe, our
responsibility is to publish what God makes
known to us and to trust that people will respond,
as they ought. But in our own house (body, lives)
we should try to establish righteousness for it is a
legacy and a priceless inheritance.

How have you ensured that future generations will walk in righteousness? How do you feel when people do not respond as zealously as you would like when you share with them the truth of God's word?

Kingdom Scribes
Seeking the Scribes Anointing

Heavenly Father, I pray for increased anointing to be bold and courageous in the things of God. Help me to speak forth what you make known to me with zealousness and resoluteness. Lord, help my generations to stand firm in truth abiding in you by faith. Govern our hearts Lord; let them be reflective of your virtues. Let them hear from you. Engrave your word on them and keep your truth in our minds. Lead us Lord by your truth. I desire that my house and I will gather as one to hear you say well done in the name of Jesus, amen.

SHAPHAN THE SCRIBE
Rock Badger

And the king commanded Hilkiah
the priest, and Ahikam the son of
Shaphan, and Achbor the son of
Michaiah, and Shaphan the scribe,
and Asahiah a servant of the
king's, saying,

2 Kings 22:12

Week 3

They shall call the people unto the
mountain; there they shall offer
sacrifices of righteousness: for
they shall suck of the abundance
of the seas, and of treasures hid in
the sand.

Deuteronomy 33:19

Shaphan the scribe chronicled the work of God in the names he gave to his sons. He made sure that they would remember what God was going to do and what God ultimately did. Each time their names were called, they would be taught about what God was going to do. As they grew, and God did it, their names served as a reminder that God alone is able to do what he says he will do.

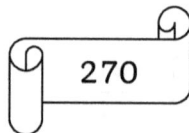

270

Shaphan son **Gemariah** name means *Jehovah has accomplished*. God said that his people would go into captivity to Babylon and it was done just as the Lord said. God put an end Judah's blatant disregard to the commands of God.

Then read Baruch in the book the words of Jeremiah in the house of the LORD, in the chamber of Gemariah the son of Shaphan the scribe, in the higher court, at the entry of the new gate of the LORD'S house, in the ears of all the people.

Jeremiah 36:10

Gemariah like his father took the words of the Lord seriously. When he heard the words of the Prophet Jeremiah read by Baruch he with others tried in vain to keep King Jehoiakim from burning the roll.

As scribes, we are to be on the side of right. It does not matter in the end how a person responses to what we say or write it does matter that we are found innocent of their blood.

When I say unto the wicked, Thou
shalt surely die; and thou givest
him not warning, nor speakest to
warn the wicked from his wicked
way, to save his life; the same
wicked man shall die in his
iniquity; but his blood will I
require at thine hand.

Ezekiel 3:18

When the Lord gives us a word, we are to deliver
it. When something is wrong, we are to speak out.
The Lord keeps an accurate record, he will reward
us according to what we have or have not done.

Confronting authority figures can at times be challenging because it can be at a high cost. How do you feel about confronting those who are over you? Do you feel intimidated? What do you do in those situations? Do you compromise your message? Avoid delivering it? What do you think God would say to you?

PRAYER

Based on the scripture below what prayer points do you desire to lift up before the Lord?

For God hath not given us the spirit of fear; but of power, and of love, and of a sound mind.

2 Timothy 1:7

You are an anointed scribe, what do you need from God in order to function in your office with a spirit of excellence? Lift up your prayer before the Lord.

SHAPHAN THE SCRIBE
Rock Badger

And the king commanded Hilkiah
the priest, and Ahikam the son of
Shaphan, and Achbor the son of
Michaiah, and Shaphan the scribe,
and Asahiah a servant of the
king's, saying,

2 Kings 22:12

Week 4

They shall call the people unto the
mountain; there they shall offer
sacrifices of righteousness: for
they shall suck of the abundance
of the seas, and of treasures hid in
the sand.

Deuteronomy 33:19

Shaphan named his other son **Elasah**, which
means whom *God has made or created*.
Elasah's role was to deliver a message from
Jeremiah to the captives that were sent to Babylon
from Jerusalem. He went with Gemariah (*Jehovah
has accomplished*) the son of Hilkiah.

These two men represented the work of God. By
using them to deliver the message to the captives,

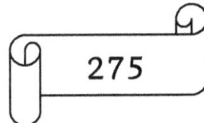

there was no doubt that all that had transpired was of the Lord. He set out to create something new and he fully accomplished it (just as he had spoken).

What was the message? That God had caused them to be carried away into captivity in Babylon. He admonished them to settle in. Build houses, plant gardens, get married and have children, and increase in number. He told them not to listen to their diviners, prophets and to not listen to ignore their dreams that were of their own making (Jeremiah 29).

God made it clear that he did not speak to them and that they were prophesying falsely in his name. God set the time of their captivity at seventy years. After that time, they would seek him with their whole heart and he would be found.

The faithfulness of **Shaphan** was clearly demonstrated. He hid the word of the Lord deep within his heart as a treasure so much so that each of his son's names was a declaration of the truth that he believed. He believed that God would fulfill his word as it was written in the book of the Law that he named his sons as a monument to its fulfillment.

The root of **Elasah's** name means *God, the one true God, Jehovah*, as well as *god-like mighty one, strength, power, and mighty heroes.* It has the same base as Jeiel (*God sweeps away*). The core meaning is prominence in a good way and belly (contemptuous) nobles or wealthy men in a bad way.

However, it also means to be a ram, which is used for food, skin dyed red (Exodus 25:5), strong man, sacrifice (Genesis 15:9), and leader, for tabernacle, pillar, doorpost or chief. The significance here is that Christ was all of these things in the godly way. He fulfilled the role of the creator and ram (sacrifice, covering, and deliverer) completely to the glory of God.

For by him were all things created,
that are in heaven, and that are in
earth, visible and invisible,
whether they be thrones, or
dominions, or principalities, or
powers: all things were created by
him, and for him:

Colossians 1:6

Christ is the ultimate strong man for he made an open display of the works of the devil. Christ is the sacrificial ram for his blood was shed so that we could have everlasting life. Christ is the one

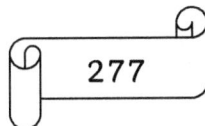

that has the sevenfold spirits of God, which include the Spirit of might. He is the chief corner stone. He is a pillar in the house of God upon which all is built. He is the preeminent one. He is the one who owns all therefore, he is abundantly wealthy.

The work of God that **Shaphan** hid in his children he openly heralded with each mention of their name. He valued it more than spoils . . . more than riches. All that he passed on through them came to pass. God word fashion a new reality for Jerusalem and Judah. His word can fashion a new reality for you as well.

As a scribe of Jehovah, it is important to hear and believe his word even if it is delayed. We are called to herald, publish, and make known what the Lord has said. We are tasked with a solemn purpose to ensure that future generations know what thus said the Lord.

How faithful are you in preserving the word that God has entrusted to you? How reliable are you to publish, herald and communicate what God has said? What blockages or obstacles do you need to address in order to be the scribe that God desires you to be?

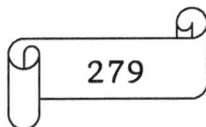

PRAYER

No one can pray for you as you can. What do you want God to do for you? He has spoken over you. He has declared a future for you. What do you need so that it comes into rich fulfillment?

It took a while for the word of God to come to fruition but it came. After the seventy years, the Lord's word once more came into completion. He can do the same for you. What do you need, patience, hope, faith, peace, zeal? Ask believing in Jesus name.

CONCLUSION

Congratulations scribe you have completed twelve months of seeking the scribes anointing. It is my earnest hope that you've discovered wonderful things about yourself, the call on your life and about our awesome God!

The richness that is woven into the names, lives and accounts of God's anointed scribes is truly mind blowing. God chooses each one carefully and for a divine purpose. He is a God that changes not; therefore, since he has chosen you, you can be assured that you fit perfectly into his master plan!

You may desire to *truly* know these scribes personally. Take time to make a case study of them. Dissect them. What they did that was virtuous, what they did that was not. Then choose what you would like to incorporate into your own life. Seek Holy Spirit for guidance so that you are confident you are walking in the path that has been laid out for you.

THE 12 SCRIBES

- Seraiah
- Jonathan
- Sheva
- Jeiel
- Elishama
- Ezra
- Shimshai
- Shebna
- Baruch
- Zadok
- Shvsha
- Shaphan

As you study them, study those around them and their other family members. When you do, you will notice how detailed God is in all that he does. He does not leave things to chance. He is a detailed planner and so he can be trusted to order your steps as he has these scribes of old.

SHAPHAN'S SONS

- Ahikam (brother has risen up)
- Gemariah (Jehovah has accomplished)
- Elasah (God has made)
- Jaazaniah (Jehovah harkens)

Continue to walk boldly in your anointing! You are a Kingdom Scribe.

THANK YOU!

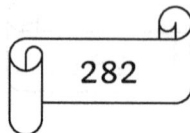

282

CHALLENGE

As a scribe, you will face writing challenges if you have not already. If you are up to the challenge, you can review each lesson keeping the following in mind:

CHALLENGES THAT SCRIBES FACE?

Writers block
Rejection
Criticism
Doubt
Fear
Trusting God
Challenges with thought expression
Clarity
Spelling
Formatting
Inspiration
Energy
*Others that are unique to you

APPLICATION

1. What did you learn from the 12 scribes that can help you address _____?

2. Studying the impact that (virtue, skill, etc.) had on the life of (name scribe) what, do you believe (whatever you identified before) will have on your life and your relationship with God?

3. What is the take home message for you?

4. What plan can you come up with to keep you moving forward as a scribe?

5. Which scribe do you feel closest to?

6. Which virtues would you like to pray in for your life and for your craft?

7. From the list of challenges, identify the skill or virtue that will aid you with overcoming the challenge.

Notes

Below jot down any thoughts, feelings, ideas that come to mind as you go through the questions or reflect on the lessons.

Kingdom Scribes
Seeking the Scribes Anointing

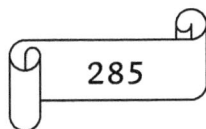

ABOUT AUTHOR

Michelle is an IPEC Certified Life Coach, Positive Prime Consultant, Christian author, publisher, copywriter, public speaker and transitional life coach at Breathe Easy Coaching. She is married to her best friend Dwain and has two handsome sons.

Contact Information

You can email Michelle at
michelle@breatheeasycoaching.com to schedule
your ELI or to discuss your coaching needs. Visit
her webpage at http://breatheeasycoaching.com

Breathe Easy FB Group
https://tinyurl.com/BreatheEasyCoachingGroup

Breathe Easy FB page
https://tinyurl.com/BreatheEasyCoachingPage

Ram Bible Studies
Website | http://rambiblestudies.com/
Join our mailing list.

Ram Bible Study FB Group
https://tinyurl.com/RamBibleStudiesFB

Overcome Secret Sins
Website | http://overcomesecretsins.com/
Join our mailing list.

Overcome Secret Sins FB Group
https://tinyurl.com/OvercomeSecretSinsFB

Global Moms in Prayer Group FB
https://tinyurl.com/GlobalMomsPrayer-Group

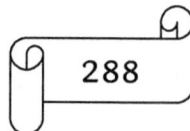

Global Moms in Prayer Group is for women who desire to pray for their children and family with other likeminded Christian women. Reference *Kingdom Scribes, Seeking the Scribes Anointing* when requesting to join the group.

ALSO BY M. J. WELCOME

NEW RELEASE

TRANSITIONING INTO FULLNESS

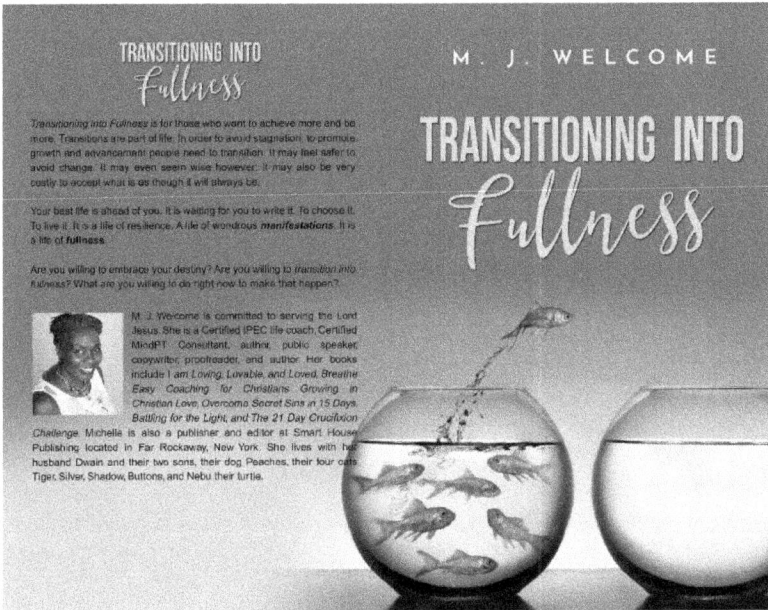

TRANSITIONING INTO
Fullness

M. J. WELCOME

TRANSITIONING INTO
Fullness

Transitioning into Fullness is for those who want to achieve more and be more. Transitions are part of life. In order to avoid stagnation, to promote growth and advancement people need to transition. It may feel safer to avoid change. It may even seem wise however, it may also be very costly to accept what is as though it will always be.

Your best life is ahead of you. It is waiting for you to write it. To choose it. To live it. It is a life of resilience. A life of wondrous *manifestations*. It is a life of *fullness*.

Are you willing to embrace your destiny? Are you willing to transition into fullness? What are you willing to do right now to make that happen.?

M. J. Welcome is committed to serving the Lord Jesus. She is a Certified iPEC life coach, Certified MindPT Consultant, author, public speaker, copywriter, proofreader, and author. Her books include I am Loving, Lovable, and Loved, Breathe Easy Coaching for Christians, Growing in Christian Love, Overcome Secret Sins in 15 Days, Battling for the Light, and The 21 Day Crucifixion Challenge. Michelle is also a publisher and editor at Smart House Publishing located in Far Rockaway, New York. She lives with her husband Dwain and their two sons, their dog Peaches, their four cats Tiger, Silver, Shadow, Buttons, and Nebu their turtle.

Life is full of transitions. In order to live a life of fullness you need to step out of your comfort zone and embrace change. The process is fraught with challenges but ***transitioning is the only way to create the life you want the way you want it!***

***Available now on Amazon.**

Kingdom Scribes
Seeking the Scribes Anointing

COMING SOON

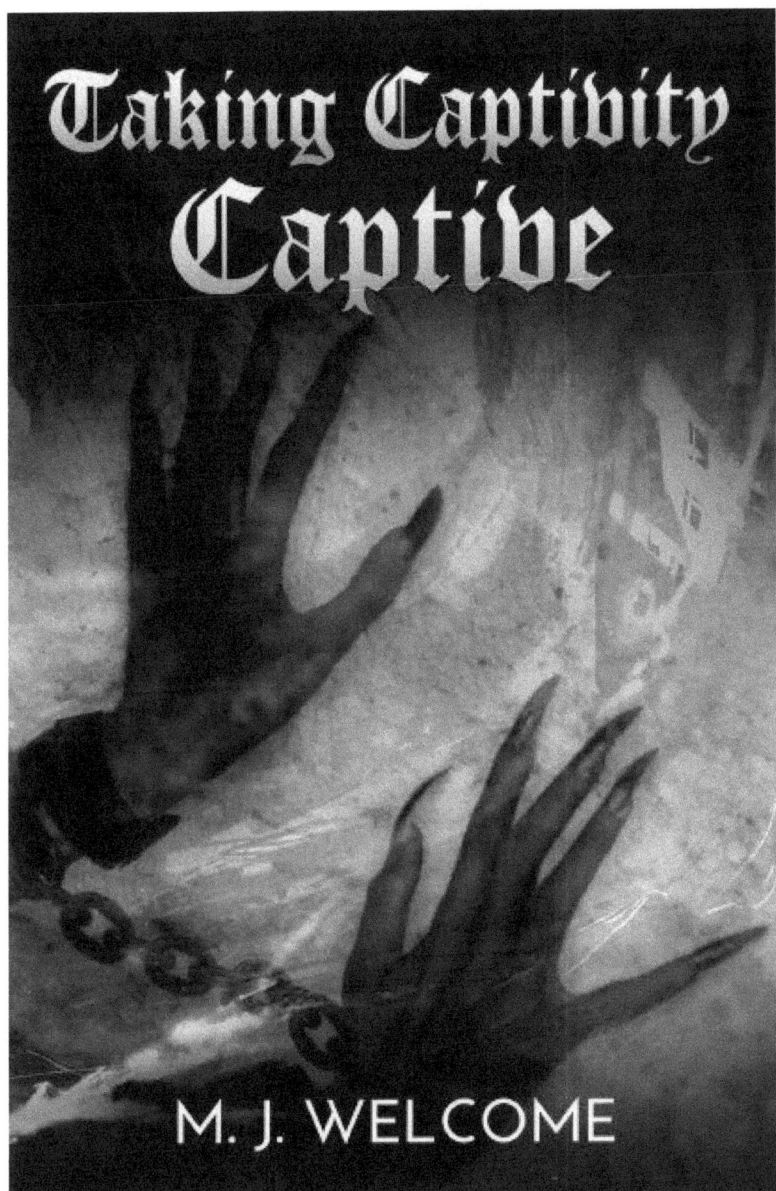

Taking Captivity Captive

M. J. WELCOME

Christ offers salvation to those who want it. Woven into the fabric of salvation is deliverance! ***Taking Captivity Captive*** is for those believers who desire to walk in greater levels of freedom. Those who want to place the enemy in shackles. Those who want to evict the strongmen from their place of comfort and influence in their lives.

If you are ready to turn, the tables on the demonic hosts of Satan then order your copy of ***Taking Captivity Captive!***

**Check Amazon now for its release!

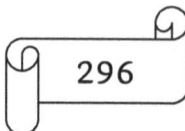

www.ingramcontent.com/pod-product-compliance
Lightning Source LLC
Chambersburg PA
CBHW060006100426
42740CB00010B/1413